D1597227

GRAND & GLORIOUS

Classic Boats of Lake Geneva

LARRY LARKIN

Larry Larkin

◆ A Sealark Publication ◆

Cataloguing in Publication

Larkin, Larry
Grand & glorious :
classic boats of Lake Geneva / Larry Larkin.

ISBN 1-55046-406-X

1. Boats and boating — Wisconsin —
Geneva, Lake — History. I. Title. II.
Title: Grand and glorious.

VM321.L37 2002   623.8'2023'0977589
2002-903454-X

Copyright © 2002 Larry Larkin

06 05 04 03 02   1 2 3 4 5

Published by
SEALARK PUBLICATIONS
W3170 County Road BB
Lake Geneva, Wisconsin
USA 53147

In association with
BOSTON MILLS PRESS
132 Main Street
Erin, Ontario
Canada N0B 1T0
Tel: 519-833-2407
Fax: 519-833-2195
www.bostonmillspress.com

Printed in Canada
Design by Gillian Stead

CONTENTS

PREFACE

he lake's earliest navigators, local Native Americans, called these pristine waters *Kishwauketoe*, meaning "clear water" or "sparkling water." John Brink, the government surveyor who mapped the area in 1835, named the lake "Geneva" because it reminded him of his home in Geneva, New York. Today, it is commonly known as Lake Geneva and it holds a well-deserved reputation for clear, spring-fed water that attracts boat lovers from all over the world.

A hundred years ago, at the turn of the previous century, the first sailboats and engine-driven boats had already appeared, but Native canoes could still be seen gliding silently along the shoreline in the pursuit of fish and game, creating hardly more than a ripple on the surface. The lifestyle evident today bears scant resemblance to that earlier era, with the lake's 26 miles of shoreline becoming the home port for a wide variety of watercraft from the most distinguished and consummate boat designers and builders of the past century.

As the early morning fog lifts, the Hathor *moves serenely through the mist.* — PHOTO BY R. BRUCE THOMPSON

This book is intended to present photographically the classic and unique powerboats and sailboats still in use on Lake Geneva. Some models are without peer, having been masterfully conceived and created. Others are historically important or are restorations worthy of note. Each vessel has some special feature, design, or unusual aspect that sets it apart from the ordinary.

It became apparent early in my research that the owners of these watercraft have a story to tell as well. Most of the boats described herein were acquired by experienced boaters who have spent time —

often much of their lives — on the water and who have gone to considerable effort and expense to study, design, build, or otherwise acquire a particular boat. To a large extent, these boats are the result of very personal decisions by their owners, the realization of their thoughts and ideas.

I want to thank the boat owners who helped make this book possible. My hope is that boat lovers everywhere will be inspired by the beauty of these classic designs, as well as by the commitment of the boats' owners, and will join in the preservation of this special heritage.

Sheets of effervescent spray accompany the 33-foot Helen A *and provide visual excitement
to match the performance as owner Bill Wrigley advances the throttle to mile-a-minute speed.* — PHOTO BY LARRY LARKIN

Chapter 1

CLASSIC AND UNIQUE BOATS

IN THE EARLY PART of the twentieth century, the hearts of many were stirred by the grandeur and deep-throated rumble of magnificent mahogany runabouts. These elegant speedboats and runabouts represent the pinnacle of creativity and craftsmanship from the era of classic high-performance boats, and by any measure would be considered outstanding examples of naval architecture. Their appearance, their touch, their sound, their smell are strongly sensual and appeal to the heart and soul of people who design, manufacture, and own these wonderful craft.

The word *classic*, as it is applied to boats, implies a timeless design, a graceful, stylish appearance, and generally refers to those boats manufactured during the first half of the twentieth century. Indeed, each of the boats described in this chapter is in some way special or unique, either a one-of-a-kind custom-built boat or one of only a few survivors of historically important models, and all may be considered classics, regardless of exact age.

Helen A

IF THERE IS ONE BOAT that personifies the classic boat era on Lake Geneva, it is the *Helen A*. Rarely seen and more rarely used during the past 50 years, it is talked about with admiration and awe whenever the fabled boats of Lake Geneva are discussed. Magnificently long at 33 feet, and lean, with a 7-foot 4-inch beam and 32-inch freeboard, the *Helen A* is a thoroughbred in every respect. The distinctive sound of its engine accelerating to top speed and the long, cantilevered bow reaching out over the waves create a unique signature recognizable for miles. The concave curvature of its bottom cuts through the water like a knife, effortlessly throwing a thin sheet of effervescent spray to each side.

The *Helen A* is without question one of the finest boats of its era. It was designed by premier raceboat designer John Hacker at the peak of his career. At 33 feet, it is among the largest of the desirable triple-cockpit runabouts, complete with the folding rear rumbleseat and with individual windshields for each cockpit. It is powered by the rare Wright Tornado V-12 aircraft engine. And it has the pedigree — custom-built for Philip Knight Wrigley, not only an accomplished businessman known for his character and integrity, but also a knowledgeable and experienced yachtsman.

The aircraft instrument panel Hacker adapted to marine use. The Wrigley boathouse is in the background.

— PHOTO BY R. BRUCE THOMPSON

Wrigley was a skilled and capable mechanic. He enlisted in the Navy in 1917, when he was 22 years old, as a Fireman, Third Class. He was discharged in 1923 with the rank of Lieutenant J.G. and was superintendent of the School for Aviation Mechanics at Great Lakes Naval Air Station. Wrigley started this mechanics' training school from scratch, buying the first Curtis flying boats with his own money. Scores of mechanics graduated from the school under his auspices, and from time to time for the rest of his life he would occasionally encounter former students all across the country who remembered well the training they had received when he was in charge of the school at Great Lakes.

Philip Wrigley never lost his love for powerful engines and fast boats, and owned a variety of watercraft during his lifetime, all interesting and unique. But the *Helen A*, named for his wife, Helen Atwater, was always special to him. He took great delight in driving it, and he was always involved in the fitting-out and launching each spring. When he was in residence at Lake Geneva, the *Helen A* was moored in front of his home, uncovered every morning, wiped down with a chamois, its chrome polished and proper flags hoisted in the best Navy tradition.

The Helen A *has a commanding
presence as its sleek, elegant hull is positioned for
spring commissioning.* — PHOTO BY R. BRUCE THOMPSON

*Suspended from the 20-ton stiff-leg
derrick, the* Helen A *is poised for launching
at the Wrigley boathouse.* — PHOTO BY R. BRUCE THOMPSON

Exquisite in her element, the tranquil appearance and graceful lines of Helen A *belie the 625-horsepower aircraft engine hidden in her engine compartment.* — PHOTO BY R. BRUCE THOMPSON

John Ludwig Hacker, the designer of the *Helen A*, is generally considered the most gifted of twentieth-century speedboat designers. His genius led to many advances in hull design, and his concepts of naval architecture and styling were the dominant influence from the early 1920s, when the gasoline engine came into its own, until his demise in the 1960s. He had a sure hand and perfect sense of proportion when it came to designing a boat's lines, and he was at the peak of his form when he designed the *Helen A*.

The *Helen A* was built by the Hacker Boat Company, located in Mount Clemens, Michigan.

Although this boat is shown in the 1939 Hacker Boat Company catalog, where it is described as a Custom Deluxe Runabout, Model 2500, it was available only on special order and this is the only one known to exist.

The boat is constructed of Honduran mahogany outer planking and Port Orford cedar inner planking fastened to oak frames. This type of construction produces a strong, light, fast boat. Indeed the boat weighs only 5,400 pounds, with 1,950 pounds being the engine. The particular Honduran mahogany used in this boat was selected for uniform color that acquires a rich honey-colored hue when varnished. The grain in the planking is exceptionally fine, straight, and uniform, producing a flawless appearance. The hardware — windshield brackets, fuel tank filler, running lights, and cleats — all show distinctive Hacker styling.

The engine is based on the Wright model T-12 Tornado liquid-cooled aircraft engine, a 12-cylinder 60-degree V configuration. It has a displacement of 1,947 cubic inches and develops 625 horsepower at 2,000 rpm in the high-compression version, which requires 100-octane aviation fuel. It was originally developed by Curtis–Wright under contract with the U.S. Navy for a water-cooled engine suitable for use in carrier-based aircraft, with the intention of replacing the First World War V-12 Liberty engine.

The fabled and rare 625-horsepower Wright Tornado aircraft engine, converted to marine use, propels the Helen A *to a speed in excess of 60 miles per hour.*
— PHOTO BY R. BRUCE THOMPSON

The engine was converted to marine applications by the Auto Engine Company of Minneapolis, Minnesota, and given the designation the Capitol Engine. The 1931 *Capitol Bulletin* describes the T-12 Tornado as "the most powerful stock marine engine available today...a dependable marine power unit with the maximum power and minimum weight of the aircraft engine... developed especially for the U.S. Navy and built under the strict supervision of Navy inspectors." The literature indicates the boat's speed with this engine is 60 miles per hour, though the local lore is that the boat goes much faster.

The boat is owned today by William Wrigley, Jr., grandson of Philip K. Wrigley and great-grandson of the founder of the William Wrigley, Jr. Company. Under Bill's stewardship the boat has been refurbished to the highest standards and is once again in the water, to everyone's delight. He has obviously inherited his grandfather's love for boats and his great-grandfather's *joie de vivre*.

Bill comments: "I first became aware of the boat when I was eight or nine years old. I always knew it was a special boat from the way my grandfather talked about it. Of all the boats he had, this boat brought him the greatest pleasure. I remember the first ride I had with him — the spray, the thunderous deep-throated roar of the engine, the total immersion in the tremendous speed of the boat at wide-open throttle.

"The boat had not been used for forty years or so, and I wanted it put in first-class condition. I asked John Buckingham and Bill Budych to go through the boat from stem to stern and to do a high-quality refurbishment but not change a thing. I wanted the boat to retain the integrity of the original design. That the boat still exists in its original configuration with the original power and with all of the original hardware and accessories is in itself remarkable, and I wanted to preserve that aspect.

"We took the engine completely apart and reassembled it piece by piece. The connecting rods and other internal parts of the engine, parts that no one ever sees, were all highly polished — a real work of art. We had gaskets specially cut, new copper water lines made where the originals had been dented or nicked. The seats were reupholstered with real leather, just as they had been originally. The goal was to put the boat back in the water and use it as it was intended to be used."

Maggie B

BILL GAGE HAS BEEN interested in boats all of his life. Assembled over many years, his collection of historic, antique, and classic boats is exceptional because of his thoughtful selections. Like many collectors, he has acquired a number of choice boats representing a particular type or style or possessing a particular design feature. In addition, Bill has studied boats extensively and amassed an extensive library of marine-related books and literature.

The *Maggie B* is a 28-foot Gar Wood runabout built in 1940. Only two of these boats were built that year, and they originally sold at the premium price of $6,300 at a time when a new Ford could be purchased for $600. The Gar Wood Boat Company converted

Beautifully restored and detailed, this 894-cubic-inch Scripps Model 302 V-12 develops 316 horsepower and powers the Maggie B *to speeds in excess of 50 miles per hour.*

— PHOTO BY R. BRUCE THOMPSON

production to the war effort in 1942, and went out of business after the war, in 1947. Thus this is a rare boat built by a premier company at the peak of the pre-war era.

There is no question that Garfield Arthur Wood was a genius. He was born in 1880, the third of 12 children of Elizabeth and Walter Wood. He was named for the Republican President and Vice-President at the time, James Garfield and Chester A. Arthur. His father was captain of a ferryboat near Minneapolis, which provided young "Gar" with his early exposure to water and watercraft, an affinity that stayed with him throughout his life.

Gar acquired an early reputation as a skilled mechanic. He made his

Sunlight illuminates the glistening mahogany hull of the Maggie B, *Bill Gage's rare 28-foot 1940 triple-cockpit Gar Wood runabout that Gar considered his flagship.* — PHOTO BY R. BRUCE THOMPSON

fortune as the inventor of the hydraulic dump mechanism used for coal and bulk material trucks in the 1920s, but he was fascinated with motorboat racing and devoted most of his life and a great deal of his fortune to the sport. Gar completely dominated speedboat racing in the United States and internationally for the next 25 years. He won every major trophy not just once, but with such repetition that opposition vanished from the scene. In 1931, his *Miss America IX* became the first boat to exceed 100 miles per hour, and his ultimate raceboat, *Miss America X,* set a speed record of 124.9 miles per hour, which stood for many years. He became known as the undisputed Speedboat King.

Gar Wood's personal wealth and his passion for the sport enabled him to maintain production long after the boat business should have closed. Every boat built by the company in the 1930s was sold at a loss — these can be viewed today as Gar Wood's gifts to the boating world. The few surviving Gar Wood boats are regarded as treasures.

Parentheses of wake and spray frame the tumblehome and the transom as the Maggie B *cuts through the water.*
— PHOTO BY R. BRUCE THOMPSON

The *Maggie B* was the flagship of Gar Wood's fleet, the ultimate refinement of his designs. A fast, elegant boat with a distinctive profile, it cuts cleanly through the water at speeds in excess of 50 miles per hour, powered by a Scripps model 302 V-12 developing 316 horsepower. This engine was the premier power plant at the time and was used only in the top-of-the-line boats.

The *Maggie B* underwent an extensive restoration program over a ten-year period, wherein the bottom was replaced, and the topsides taken down to the bare wood and refinished with multiple coats of marine varnish. The interior has been reupholstered with genuine leather. The powerful Scripts engine was completely disassembled and overhauled. The engine restoration was so thorough it included replacement of the engine's main bearings and re-heat treatment of the crankshaft.

Gar Wood left a legacy of boats that may never be equaled. The few that survive, such as the *Maggie B,* have become highly desired classics because of their design, styling, and performance and are recognized as among the best of their day.

Alouette

THE *Alouette*, MEANING "LARK" in French, is a custom-built, one-of-a-kind design based on traditional lines but built with modern materials and equipment. It is not a reproduction but a new design incorporating classic elements, especially from the post-World War II period.

The underwater portion of the hull is based on an air-sea rescue boat designed to provide a smooth, fast ride in rough water for the rescue of downed aviators. The underbody features slightly convex sections forward, and a relatively straight run aft with little dead rise that makes for good high-speed performance. The above-water part of the boat has the traditional John Hacker profile from the post-war period. This is characterized by slightly more freeboard than on his earlier boats, while retaining the tumblehome of the sides aft and the slight reverse rake of the transom, which are characteristic of boats from this era.

I remember when I was a young boy admiring the beautiful lines of the elegant mahogany speedboats from the thirties and forties. I thought they were the epitome of design, especially the long triple-cockpit models.

About 1980, I met Tom Flood, who had worked at the original Hacker Boat Company in Mount Clemens, Michigan in the 1940s. He had saved some

Alouette's twin Mercruiser 502 engines idle with a low rumble as she moves forward toward open water. — PHOTO BY R. BRUCE THOMPSON

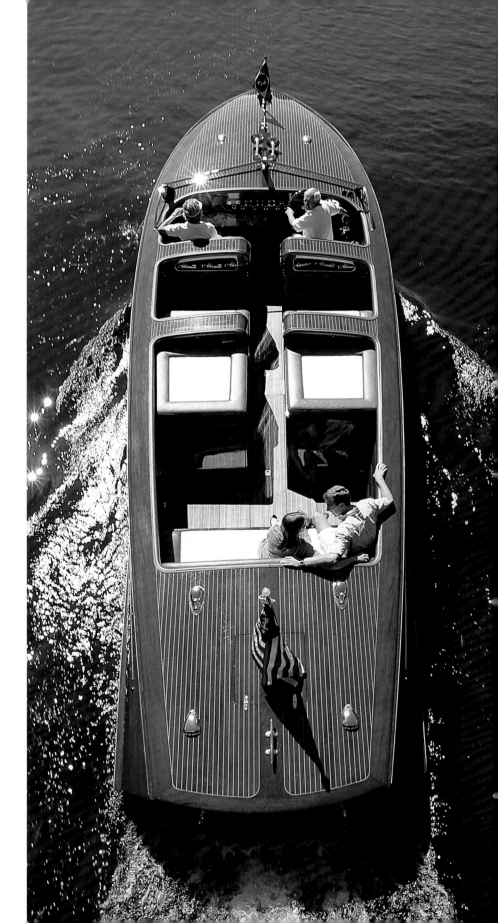

drawings from this period that showed the characteristic Hacker lines and looked terrific. I contacted naval architect Charlie Jannace, of Black Fin fame, and asked him to design a boat that would have a smooth ride in rough water and would incorporate the classic Hacker look from the post-war period with an interior that would be user-friendly. We ended up with a classically styled 33-foot boat with clean underwater lines designed to perform well at speed but with a slightly convex shape in the bow for a cushioned ride. The boat displaced 9,000 pounds and would be powered by twin Mercruiser 502 engines with a design speed of 60 miles per hour!

Then I found a remarkable builder in Gravenhurst, in the Muskoka Lakes region of Ontario, Canada. Mike Windsor had just finished a boat for the Prime Minister of Canada. He sawed his planks from raw timbers so that the grain and color matched, and he saved the ends of the planks and cut the screw plugs from them so that they also matched. He made his own patterns for casting the boat's windshield and fittings, and he was willing to build a traditional double-plank bottom with rubber sealer between the layers. Everything he said was consistent and hung together.

The rich mahogany and navy blue leather upholstery creates a unified harmony with Lake Geneva's clear blue water.
— PHOTO SUE LARKIN

"For me, this was a dream job," says Mike Windsor. "I think Larry found what he was looking for in the way of a builder, as I did with him as a patron: a man with a vision and belief in my abilities. I loved doing this project because everything was done first class. The best materials were used from stem to stern. Honduran mahogany was used for the double-planked hull, and Burmese teak inlaid with holly for the deck, The windshield, gas tank covers, the vents in the side of the engine compartment, deck and air vents are authentic Hacker designs and are all typical of those used in 1940s. Nothing was held back. It inspired and challenged all of us to do the very best job possible."

Close inspection of the seams and joints in the hull planking attests to Mike's craftsmanship. To the extent we have built a classic boat it is to the credit of John Hacker, Charlie Jannace and Mike Windsor. My role was simply the enabler with the vision. I hope the boat will grow in favor as it ages and that, through the *Alouette*, I can leave a model of marine architecture for future generations to enjoy and appreciate: a craft of powerful lines whose beauty is born of speed, a boat for the next millennium that incorporates the best of the past.

The powerful and pleasing design influence of John Hacker is flawlessly manifested as Alouette *skims the surface of the water with style and speed.* — PHOTO BY FRED GELDERMANN

The precise fit of the frames is a testament to the extraordinary skills of Muskoka Lakes boatbuilder Mike Windsor.
— PHOTO BY MIKE WINDSOR

Like a butterfly emerging from its cocoon, the Alouette *is rolled into daylight for the first time. Responding to the question "How do you feel at this moment?" builder Mike Windsor responded, "It is thrilling to see it come out the big door in one piece because for the last two years the parts have been carried in through the side door, board by board."*
— PHOTO BY ED WEED

Moonglade

Moonglade, OWNED BY KENT SHODEEN, is a Stan-Craft torpedo-styled speedster built in 1998. The name refers to the reflection of the moon's light on the surface of the water. *Moonglade* is the first of the new series of torpedo speedsters. A 420-horsepower 8.2-liter Mercruiser V-8 propels the 29-foot-long, 7-foot-beam, 5,000-pound boat to speeds in excess of 50 miles per hour.

Stan-Craft was founded by Stanley C. Young in 1933 on the shores of Flathead Lake in Montana. From the beginning, they specialized in beautiful mahogany runabouts and cruisers. Today the firm is owned by Syd Young, son of the founder, and is currently located in Post Falls, Idaho. In the 69 years since the firm was founded, father and son have built over 500 boats, from 21 feet to 36 feet.

Syd Young comments: "The boats we built in the early days, especially before the war, had relatively flat bottoms aft and hollow sections forward to get more speed from the limited power available. These were large, expensive boats, usually the triple-cockpit style. Today we have all kinds of power, so the trick is to keep the classic look and gracefulness of these boats yet get them to perform well and have a smooth ride."

Although Stan-Craft has built many successful boats, the torpedo speedster is a unique boat and a specialty of the house. Stan Young designed the first tapered-stern 22-foot double-cockpit runabout, which

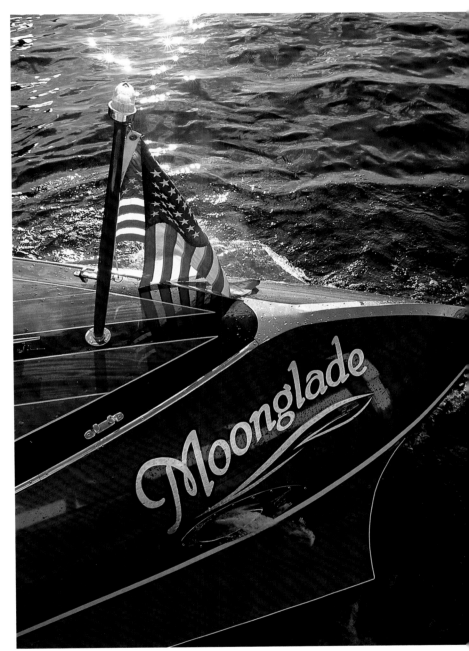

The water-cooled exhaust exits the hull on both sides aft through chrome-plated, teardrop-shaped ports.
— PHOTO BY R. BRUCE THOMPSON

he called a Torpedo, in 1943 and completed construction of the prototype in 1946. Stan, and later son Syd, continued to develop the torpedo-styled boat in various lengths, cockpit configurations, and under-body shapes. According to Syd, "Along the way, we decided to try to reach a new market with something more provocative. We built a 25-foot speedster with two cockpits. A speedster is driven from the cockpit behind the engine, and you have most of the boat in front of you. The rear cockpit of this boat was a little cramped, so we stretched the boat to 26 feet. Then we decided to combine the torpedo-styled hull with the speedster-styled interior and came up with *Moonglade*. There are two cockpits aft with a cockpit forward in the form of a rumbleseat that can be closed up.

"Over the past 70 years we've continually refined this hull making subtle line changes until we have it just about perfect, to the point that now it does everything you could expect a boat to do. It has all the characteristics most appreciated by boaters: a soft entry, fabulous turning ability, and with no bad habits. It gets up without rearing in the bow and lays flat. It has more of a tendency to levitate horizontally and ride on its lines. The deep 50-to-55-degree entry at the bow gives it a sharp entry, but the bottom quickly transitions to a very shallow seven-to-eight-degree dead rise at the stern.

"The bottom comes back full width to the stern, while the above-water portion of the hull tapers back toward the centerline. This results in a step on each side at the stern that significantly extends the planing surface to each side of the boat and provides support in tight turns. But with the spray shield extended aft on both sides, the stern step is hardly noticeable.

"It turned out like magic. It cuts sharply, it rides smoothly. We went through a dozen different designs over the past ten years, making small adjustments to improve the performance of the bottom, trying to provide an exceptionally smooth ride while at the same time providing high performance; that is, high-speed maneuverability, turning, cutting. I think we are at the point that I don't see how it could be improved. It rides and handles just beautifully. And it turns unbelievably quickly, with a very tight radius."

Moonglade's owner, Kent Shodeen, recalls, "When I first saw the *Moonglade* in Coeur d'Alene, Idaho, I knew it was special. Syd Young took us for a demonstration ride that was really something! I liked the way it handled. It is fast — really fast! It lays out on top of the water. It rides well. It cuts thorough the waves easily. It has a firm foot in the water. When you turn the wheel left or right, the boat responds immediately, with amazingly sharp turns even at top speed. And I like the way it looks. What else is there? It's a special boat!"

AT LEFT: *Kent Shodeen's* Moonglade, *a 28-foot Stan-Craft torpedo-stern speedster, gives new meaning to the phrase "high-speed performance."* — PHOTO BY R. BRUCE THOMPSON

Koukla Moo

Ernie Cochanis' 30-foot 1959 Shepherd,
Koukla Moo, *offers stylish transportation.*

— PHOTO BY R. BRUCE THOMPSON

Koukla Moo IS A 30-FOOT SHEPHERD utility built in 1959. It is owned by Ernie Cochanis, who acquired the boat in 1985. Ernie notes, "The boat had been sitting for five years in the old Geneva Lake Boat Company storage building right next door to my home. It had great lines and it was a woody and it just enthralled me. It was such a large boat and twin Chrysler hemis powered it. So I bought it."

The Shepherd Boat Company was started by Lloyd H. Shepherd in 1931, in Beamsville, Ontario, Canada. He was a flamboyant, outgoing proprietor who was a businessman first and a boatbuilder second. An excellent salesman, he single-handedly built the company from its initial start-up to its status as a significant boatbuilder during its 40-year existence. Shep, as his friends called him, was meticulous about his business. He would fly to Honduras to personally select mahogany for his boats. Quality and craftsmanship were key to his reputation.

Shepherd actually started his business in the early 1920s, manufacturing wooden trailers and wood trim for automobiles, but by the early 1930s he was manufacturing rowboats, canoes, and small outboards. In 1934 Shepherd hired Earl Barnes, a well-known Canadian naval architect from the Muskoka Lakes region, to design a line of larger inboard motorboats. The earliest boats were 17-foot and 23-foot utilities that were practical open boats with substantial freeboard for the rough waters in the area. A fire in 1939 forced the company to relocate in the town of Niagara-on-the-Lake, at the mouth of the Niagara River.

After the war, the company expanded and produced a line of 27-foot twin-engine runabouts — large, heavy speedboats. In the early 1950s the 27-foot model was "stretched" to produce a 30-foot express cabin cruiser, a type of boat known as a "commuter." This boat was originally intended to have an enclosed cabin, but as it was being built, before the cabin was put on, Shepherd thought it looked good as an open boat, so he completed the boat as a huge speedboat. The area behind the captain's seat already had a refrigerator, sink, serving counters and storage cabinets built in, all items usually found in a cabin cruiser but not usually found in an open utility-style boat. Shepherd left them in place.

These 30-foot boats were enormous, with a 10-foot beam and weighing 4 tons. They were powered originally by twin Chrysler V-8 hemis with V-drive, which allowed the engines to be placed in the stern of the boat. Top speed was 38 miles per hour.

The well-designed instrument panel and engine controls monitor Koukla Moo's *performance.* — PHOTO BY R. BRUCE THOMPSON

The boats were very solidly built — "built like a rock" was an expression frequently used to describe them. They are rare, only 14 were built. This boat, built in 1959, is number 13 in the series. The design is characteristic of all Shepherd boats, with high freeboard and relatively straight line styling. Most of the hardware and fittings were unique to Shepherd and were manufactured by the Shepherd Boat Company. The air vents, again characteristic of Shepherd, were handcarved out of mahogany.

Ernie Cochanis remembers: "I sent the boat to Canada to have it redone. I had the engines replaced with the big block Chevy 454s because parts for the original Chrysler hemis were no longer available. On the way back, the Canadian customs officials stopped the boat at the border and didn't want to let it pass. They thought it was a Canadian national treasure.

"I truly enjoy going out in the boat. It's a real thrill to have people wave and give a thumbs up. And the best part is, it doesn't matter how many people you have in the boat, it still goes fast and planes well."

Glen Fern

THE *Glen Fern*, A 2000 BOESCH model 680 Costa Brava, is owned by Bob and Joan Clifford. Boesch boats are not common in the United States, the manufacturer, Boesch Motorboats is headquartered in Kilchberg, on the shores of Lake Zurich, in Switzerland. The company was founded in 1920 by Jacob Boesch, with Jacob's son Walter coming into the business 1928. He brought together the union of timeless craftsmanship and meticulously developed innovation that characterizes Boesch today.

Such was the early success of the business that by 1930 the Swiss were cruising Lake Zurich in stylish, deep-chestnut-tinted speedboats they called Autoboats because they seemed so much like waterborne sportscars.

Boesch covers a solid mahogany frame in wide multiple planks of laminated construction. The hull is then coated with seven applications of epoxy followed by four layers of polyurethane varnish. As a result, Boesch runabouts glow with all the deep-grained richness of traditional mahogany boats but are much stronger, more rigid, and more easily maintained than wooden craft manufactured using traditional methods.

Three craftsmen are assigned to the construction of each hull, working in a calm, resolute manner. The structure and planking are put in place, then the craft is held until an order comes in, at which time the boat is completed. That way every Boesch boat can be customized to the owner's desires. Virtually any feature of the boat can be modified as long as the boat's signature lines are not compromised. Hardware and other fittings are machined out of solid bronze billets and then chrome-plated. Engines are the latest Mercruiser V-8s with electronic controls and fuel injection. As Boesch says, "Quite simply, we build the boats to last forever."

Bob Clifford: "We first saw these boats at Grand Craft in Holland, Michigan, when we were talking with them about a motor launch for Lake Geneva. I thought they were well made and had a nice line to them. The Swiss quest for perfection came through in the design and construction of the boat."

The functional requirements of the instrument panel are enhanced by the arrangement of engine controls.

— PHOTO BY R. BRUCE THOMPSON

Joan and Bob Clifford cruise in Glen Fern, *a sleek and stylish 22-foot Boesch Costa Brava runabout.*
The lush garden surrounding their recently restored 1911 home is seen in the background.
— PHOTO BY R. BRUCE THOMPSON

Riva

TO BOATING ENTHUSIASTS, the name Riva evokes the image of speed manifested with elegant Italian styling. Indeed, these boats are some of the most eye-catching craft to be built in recent years. The Riva is the benchmark for European craftsmanship in terms of finish, elegance, and performance in contemporary powerboating.

In 1842 Pietro Riva was 24 years old and had worked as a general craftsman, turning his hand to various trades, including boat repairs on and around Lake Como, in Northern Italy, when he was asked to repair two storm-damaged boats in Sarnico, on the banks of the Oglio River, a location now synonymous with the Riva name. With the reputation this work established for him, young Pietro continued in the boat-repair business and, in a short time, established a boat yard at Sarnico, where he was commissioned to build a fishing boat in the true "Como" fashion. The new company went on to become a supplier of elegant and luxurious powercraft.

In the early 1950s, fifth-generation Carlo Riva foresaw a rebirth of interest in pleasure boating and set out to design and build the world's finest luxury speedboats. He wanted to devise a way to eliminate leaks and cracks in the seams between the planks caused by the swelling and shrinking of the wood. He felt fiberglass was not the total answer, and plywood did not fill the bill, so he devised a method of construction he called "armored lamination." The side of the boat is completely glued up in one piece on a fixture, then attached to the boat's frames. All the laminations used for the side were of Honduran mahogany, while the frames and stringers were made of select fir and were also laminated rather than being cut out of solid lumber.

Carlo was a perfectionist, and in building his boats he insisted on the finest wood. Only 20 percent of the lumber Riva orders is deemed acceptable, the balance being returned to the supplier. The selected lumber is placed in temperature- and humidity-controlled storage for at least three years before it is used. For consistency of color and finish, Carlo insisted that only planks from the same tree be used on each boat. Indeed, the mahogany is so well matched that the seams are almost invisible, and planks run from bow to stern without joints. Each Riva receives nine layers of hand-rubbed varnish, a process that takes over two months to perform. Riva also makes all its own hardware and fittings, and everything is designed for saltwater operation. Each boat is put through a 20-hour test program at the factory before being shipped to the customer.

With their classic wooden construction and exemplary finish, they captured the imagination of royalty and rapidly achieved the prestige they still hold to this day. And, yes, there are Rivas on Lake Geneva.

Owned by Michael Nicholas, this Aquarama Special is powered by twin 454-cubic-inch Crusader engines. In the background is the Nicholas home. — PHOTO BY R. BRUCE THOMPSON

Aquarama Special

THIS RIVA IS OWNED BY Michael Nicholas. It is a 1990 Aquarama Special. Aquarama means "View of the Sea," while Special refers to its length and is identifiable by the recess in the transom and rear deck. The 28-foot-long boat weighs 7,000 pounds and can attain a speed of 55 miles per hour.

According to Mike, "When the lake is smooth, the boat goes as if it were riding on glass. I saw a number of Rivas in Monaco and northern Italy when we were visiting a few years ago. There were probably 50 of them lined up in Monte Carlo. I thought they were the most beautiful boats I had seen and decided to try to find one. About three years ago, a broker who specialized in Rivas helped me find one in Florida. I bought it in March of 1999 and sent it to Clayton, New York, to be refinished and then brought it to Lake Geneva. I love the Italian styling, the curved windshield, the way the curve of the deck tapers into the stern. The side of the boat, over 28 feet long, is laid up on fixtures and glued together so the seams between the planks are virtually invisible. It is an elegant method of construction used by no one else in the world."

Esco Pazzo, *Charles Johnston's 28-foot 1969 Riva Super Aquarama, performs at speed.* — PHOTO BY LARRY LARKIN

Esco Pazzo

THIS RIVA, *Esco Pazzo*, IS OWNED BY Charles Johnston. It is a 28-foot twin-engine 1969 Super Aquarama, which can be identified by the solid transom and rear deck.

"The first time I ever saw a Riva, I was sitting on the dock at my house admiring another Lake Geneva sunset," Charles recalls. "I saw a boat approaching that made my jaw drop. It looked like a piece of artwork floating by, with its combination of mahogany, leather, curved windshield, glistening chrome, and sculpted stern. As it passed by, I saw the letters R-i-v-a on its hull. I was immediately bitten by the Riva bug.

Riva instrument panel and engine controls show the impeccable attention to detail.

— PHOTO BY LARRY LARKIN

"The boat was obviously beautiful, but I was skeptical that it could also be durable and reliable, two qualities I've learned over 30 years of boating are absolute necessities in a boat. I began to research Riva and became fascinated with the legend of Carlo Riva and the three generations of Rivas, the first of whom began building fishing boats in Italy in 1842.

"After learning all of this, I was ready to buy a Riva. While I looked up each of the models Riva manufactured, I decided to focus my attention on their top-of-the-line model, the Aquarama, which is also their most famous boat. My search took me all over the country, from Lake Tahoe to New York. My friends and family thought I was crazy, but I was on a mission to find the perfect Riva.

"I found my boat up in the Finger Lakes area of upstate New York. It is a 1969 Super Aquarama powered by twin 454-cubic-inch Crusader engines, each developing 350 horsepower. The boat is hull number 338 out of about 700 in the Aquarama series and was originally delivered to financier Gerald Tsai of New York City. When I bought the boat, its name was *Esco Pazzo*. I had no idea what that meant until a year after I bought the boat. A good friend of ours, who is Italian, came to visit and went for a ride in the boat, and asked the name of it. She said a literal translation is 'I must be crazy.' Somehow, after all of this, it seems like an appropriate name.

"When I entered it in its first and probably only boat show at Lake Geneva, it won People's Choice. The boat was bought to be used, and we enjoy it every chance we get and still find it an absolute delight to run."

Modern Production Hackercraft

JOHN LUDWIG HACKER'S NAME appears often in these pages. He was born in Detroit on May 24, 1877, and died in 1961. From childhood, he haunted Detroit's waterfront and boat yards, and his life and career spanned what is generally considered to be the classic era of mahogany speedboats. Indeed, Hacker's concepts of hull design were the dominant influence in runabouts from the early 1920s, when the gasoline engine came into its own, until the wooden speedboat era ended with the introduction of fiberglass in the late 1950s.

Around 1900, Hacker realized that to go fast his boats would have to plane on top of the water rather than go through the water. He developed a design for a hull that would produce maximum speed and efficiency without squatting, a problem common to most speedboats of the period, which were long and narrow with rounded bilges. As a result, Hacker boats rode much more level than other boats and it was a smoother ride. They laid out over the water and didn't pound.

Although John Hacker had a romance with racing boats, he was a prolific naval architect who created more than a thousand designs during his lifetime, most of them custom boats ranging from modest skiffs, runabouts, cruisers and commuters to military personnel carriers and elegant yachts. He designed his boats for comfort as well as good looks and speed. In Hacker designs, the sheer line drops off a little as it goes to the bow, which adds a lot to the style. The lines and proportions of a Hacker design look as good today as they did 50 years ago when they were new.

During the Great Depression, John Hacker left the Hacker Boat Company, though it continued to operate until it went out of business two decades later. Meanwhile, Hacker continued to design boats into the early 1960s. These boats were often custom one-of-a-kind boats built for discriminating owners. Hackercrafts are probably the rarest of the classic inboard runabouts from the 1930s, since so few of them were built. A vintage Hackercraft is a prized possession, highly regarded for its elegant lines and graceful form.

Today, in the small Lake George village of Silver Bay, in upstate New York, Hackercrafts are still being built in the Hacker style. Bill Morgan, the driving force behind the modern Hackercraft, has made some changes to the early Hacker designs. But some aspects of the boats remain unchanged. The use of Honduran mahogany, a minimum of 12 coats of hand-rubbed varnish, and traditional hardware produce a modern craft reminiscent of the early Hackers.

A number of these modern Hackercrafts built of wood by the reborn Hacker Boat Company in Silver Bay, New York, have been brought to Lake Geneva. This is due in part to the size of the lake and the need for a longer boat to give a comfortable ride. But in greater part it is due to a renewed appreciation of this type of historic watercraft.

The Eagle, *Tara and Cedric Blazer's 31-foot 1990 twin-engine Hackercraft,*
is aptly described as a "wood racer." — PHOTO BY R. BRUCE THOMPSON

Eagle

THE *Eagle*, CEDRIC AND TARA BLAZER'S 1990 custom-built Hackercraft is modeled after a 1930s design by John Hacker and is powered by twin 270-cubic-inch Crusader V-6s. Cedric Blazer recalls the occasion when he first saw the boat in Door County, near Sturgeon Bay, Wisconsin: "When I saw this boat, I thought it was beautiful. I watched it every summer for three years, and when it became available, I bought it. The only place for a boat like this is on Lake Geneva. So after I bought the boat, I bought a summer home on Lake Geneva so I would have a place to keep it."

Miss Dixie

Miss Dixie *is a handsome 29-foot sport boat custom-built by Hackercraft in 1998 especially for*
Dixie and Kenneth Malek. The 4,800-pound craft is powered by a Crusader 502-cubic-inch engine
and attains a speed in excess of 50 miles per hour. — PHOTO BY R. BRUCE THOMPSON

Mondo

The polished, custom-built 26-foot 1996 Hackercraft Mondo *is pictured with Joan Wegner at the helm in front of her lakeshore home. The multi-colored* Mondo *name represents the flavors of her company's popular line of soft drinks. According to Joan's son, Chuck Wegner, "It's a dream boat. The bow cuts through the waves and the boat lays out very well. And we love the beauty and the feel of the wood."* — PHOTO BY R. BRUCE THOMPSON

Joyce and Matthew Walsh relaxing in front of their home in Dingle, *an attractive boat from any angle.* — PHOTO BY R. BRUCE THOMPSON

Dingle

"I always thought Hacker boats had wonderful lines, especially when they were in the water," *Dingle* owner Matthew Walsh explains. "I remember seeing a Gage-Hacker many years ago and liked the way that boat looked. When Bill Morgan began to build Hacker boats in upstate New York, I went to the factory to see what they were doing. I had the *Dingle* specially built. This 24-foot size rides marvelously on Lake Geneva. It's just the right size for this lake. The hull design just sheds waves."

Star Chaser

Star Chaser is a custom-designed 29-foot raceboat being built for Dean L. Griffith by Syd Young of Juliette Corporation in Post Falls, Idaho. Although the basic style is typical of a gentlemen's racer from the late 1920s, which featured the steering wheel in the cockpit just aft of the engine, the underwater hull form is anything but gentlemanly. It incorporates elements from Gar Wood's famous *Miss America X*, built in 1932 to win the Harmsworth Trophy, the most prestigious prize at that time in unlimited speedboat racing, and notable for setting the world water speed record of 134 miles per hour.

Star Chaser is designed for mile-a-minute speed. Propulsion is provided by twin Mercruiser 350-cubic-inch. Black Scorpion V-8 engines that have been specially modified and detailed by engine expert Larry

With the first of many coats of varnish applied, but lacking hardware, Star Chaser *emerges briefly from Syd Young's construction shed in May 2002. The design elements incorporated from* Miss America X *can be seen in the bow, sheer, and transom.*

— PHOTO BY SYD YOUNG

Mayea of Mayea Boat Works, Fair Haven, Michigan, to boost their performance to the 400-horsepower realm. "Working as a team with Dean and Syd to build this boat has made it an exciting project," Larry enthused. "In Dean we have an owner who knows exactly what he wants and who is involved in every detail: the windshield design, the deck layout, and with all the other special features that make this boat unique." Syd Young agrees, "It was a joy to build this boat. Although it incorporates elements from other boats, this boat is special. There are only two or three twin-engine gentlemen's racers in the world, and none will perform like this one."

Dean Griffith summed up the concept: "In many ways, this boat is symbolic of the vision I have had all my life. I've tried to inspire young people to become more than they thought they could be; to have stars in their eyes, to reach for the stars! I've always liked what the Apostle Paul said in his letter to the Ephesians: '...to accomplish more than we can imagine, beyond our wildest dreams.' That's why I built this boat, to challenge the designer and the builder to do something that hadn't been done before, to reach beyond the ordinary, and that's why I chose the name *Star Chaser*."

Chapter 2

POPULAR
RUNABOUTS AND UTILITIES

A number of boatbuilders have been located around the shore of Lake Geneva at different times in the past. The Napper Boat Company, located in Lake Geneva, and the Palmer Boat Company of Fontana are long gone. The marketplace changed irrevocably as new styles and types of boats developed and made their products obsolete. However, three companies, Gage-Hacker, Globe, and Streblow, manufactured motorboats in significant numbers and of such creditable design that the boats are now recognized as American classics. Of these, the one organization that continues to manufacture boats and that has been the most successful in terms of numbers of boats built and owner loyalty is the Streblow Boat Company.

AT LEFT: *July 2001 – a roar to remember! Randy Streblow, flying a white pennant, leads the fleet as 50 Streblows participate in a rally at full throttle for a non-stop run down the entire 7-mile length of the lake.*
— PHOTO BY R. BRUCE THOMPSON

Streblow owners wait for the fog to lift just before the rally.

Streblow

LARRY STREBLOW, FOUNDER and patriarch of Streblow Boat Company, has been "fooling around with boats" all his life. Larry was born with the instinct to build things and with an affinity for wood likely inherited from his father, who was still building violins when he was 86 years old. Larry recalls, "My father gave me a rowboat when I was eleven years old. Within two weeks I had remodeled it with a bicycle-pedaling apparatus and a water wheel."

Larry Streblow began his professional career as a draftsman and eventually became a design engineer for a variety of marine and furniture companies. "I built my first boat in 1947, just for the fun of it," he says, "and then I got hung up on my hobby. Building boats is an art. But it isn't art alone. It is science as

well. It's a balanced combination of the two. All these boats are worked out first on drawings with lines and offsets. After we've determined what we want, then we go to lofting. All our boats are built directly off our lofting, which is done on heavy plywood — a permanent material that works well over time.

"The other things are the workmanship and the materials we use. It's a combination of everything we do. Our goal is to use the best materials, the best of everything there is. As long as there are those who appreciate fine wood and excellent craftsmanship, there will always be a place for Streblow boats."

The hobby became a business in 1951 and was incorporated in 1954. In the early days of the company, they built a variety of outboard- and

The Streblow signature white recurve accents the sides of the boats. — PHOTO BY KRIS STREBLOW

inboard-powered boats from 14 to 28 feet. Along the way, they restored a good many boats and built specialized boats such as racing hydro-planes.

In 1961, Larry was joined by his son, Randy, and Randy's wife, Cathy. They decided to concentrate on building fewer but larger inboards with more elaborate appointments. They have remained a small family-owned company, joined in 1987 by Randy's daughter, Kris. Today, Randy and Kris look after the business, with Randy doing most of the actual construction. Working with Steve Horton, a longtime employee, they turn out only a handful of carefully built boats each year.

Randy Streblow talks warmly about his boats: "The whole boat is a Streblow design. The transom, bottom and bow are unique to these boats. Everything is custom-made: the hardware, lifting rings, and cleats are all special. Although we won't change the basic hull form and the bottom, every boat is custom-designed. Each owner wants special features, such as teak deck, swim platform, and sometimes unique seating arrangements. We build what the customer wants.

"We used to build smaller boats, but they didn't ride well on the waves on Lake Geneva. A 23-foot boat is about as small as you can go. Most of our boats today are 26 and 28 feet, powered by 8.1-liter engines. They go about 55 miles per hour. Today, the boats are wider, the bottom line straighter, the interiors more modern and plush, the ride softer, and they have the power and ability to go considerably faster. We've made changes to the hull over the years. We've

Lynn McKeahey starts the engine for the Streblow rally as her dog, Maddie, checks the starboard quarter.

The combined effect of the many wakes provided both a challenge and a thrill as rally participants tried to maintain course and speed through the heavy chop.

— PHOTOS BY SPENCER WEBER

Randy Streblow in El Do VIII, *his personal boat, surrounded by other Streblows. This is the only triple-cockpit style Streblow has built.*
— PHOTO BY TOM RAMSEY

dropped the forefoot and increased the deck crown. We've got about as much vee in the bow as you can have. The boat rides very smoothly. There are no other boats like them. It is an amazing feeling when you create something beautiful and praiseworthy out of a few pieces of wood and metal."

Kris Streblow adds, "My grandfather and my father were always concerned with quality, and it became a Streblow hallmark. Streblows are known far and wide for their rock-solid, durable construction. We feel very loyal to our customers and a real attachment to all our boats. From the

moment we start on one, we give it all our attention. And when the boat leaves, it is still part of us." Indeed, more than one customer has said that when they talked with Randy about a boat, they felt he was interviewing them to see if they were worthy of owning a Streblow.

"We have a five-year warranty," states Randy, "but if anything ever goes wrong that's our fault, we take care of it."

Randy Streblow, fitting a chine to the latest Streblow hull, shows his artistry with a plane.
— PHOTO BY R. BRUCE THOMPSON

This scenic lagoon is the perfect setting for Marsha and Bob Silverstein's 23-foot 1961 Streblow, the last of the models with fins that reflect the automotive styling of the era. — PHOTO BY R. BRUCE THOMPSON

Sun-E-Skies, *Larry Liebovich's 28-foot 2001 Streblow is the latest model with twin Crusader 502 engines and direct drive.*

— PHOTO BY R. BRUCE THOMPSON

*Corresponding beauty, JimBo, Helga and Jim Pearson's
23-foot 1983 Streblow, with their award-winning flower
garden in the background.*

— PHOTO BY R. BRUCE THOMPSON

*The real McCoy exists — Zen Dream,
Nancy McCoy and Mark Scharres's 20-foot 1979 Streblow.
Nancy had dreamed of owning a Streblow since she was 14.*

— PHOTO BY LARRY LARKIN

Like racing torpedoes, these two Gage-Hackers, Flapjack *and* Fireball, *cut through the water at full speed.*
— PHOTO BY R. BRUCE THOMPSON

Gage-Hacker

GAGE-HACKER BOATS WERE DESIGNED especially for Lake Geneva and built by Gage Marine starting in 1958, at a time when virtually all the large boat manufacturers were converting to fiberglass. As Bill Gage recalls: "My father, Russ, and I started thinking about building a line of boats designed especially for Lake Geneva in the late 1950s. We believed there was a market on Lake Geneva for mahogany speedboats, even with fiberglass boats becoming common. When the wind picks up, this lake gets a chop or roughness that made most of the boats then on the market slap or pound the waves with a resulting rough ride. We had a 26-foot Hacker-designed boat called the *Gypsy* that had convex sections on the underwater portion of the hull forward and carried a significant amount of dead rise back to the transom. This boat was an easy-riding boat that performed well in the Lake Geneva chop. It did not manifest any of the bottom problems that tended to plague boats built by other manufacturers.

"Our vision was to build a classic-styled boat with modern engines and controls so it would look attractive and be easy to drive. We wanted to capture the easy-riding capabilities of that 26-foot Hacker we had. John Ludwig Hacker was still designing boats, so I went to see him to work with him on a design. That was in June 1960, when he was 83 years old. He was working in a musty office in an old building in downtown Detroit with his younger brother, who was working with him as his draftsman. John was still committed to his life's work. He still knew all about the calculations associated with his boats. It turned out that he had been working on a design for a 22-foot boat that would work well for us, so we continued to develop that design. His brother sat at the drafting table translating the ideas we discussed into working drawings. This was the last design that Hacker did. He died shortly afterward.

"To test the design, to see if the characteristics we desired would be realized in the finished boat, we had a number of models handmade of an existing design and also proposed designs. We took them to the University of Michigan at Ann Arbor, where they had a naval architecture department and a towing tank. We ran the first model, which was based on an existing boat, and observed that it duplicated in miniature the planing angle and performance of that boat. We tested the model of the proposed design and then modified the model slightly to see how that would change the performance. We repeated the process until we were satisfied that we had the underwater sections we were looking for. It was quite an experience to ride on the towing platform as it moved along the tank, leaning over almost upside-down with our heads just above the water to study the bow wave and the angle the model exhibited. This design work paid off because the full-sized boats maintained the proper planing angle at all speeds, and the driver had excellent visibility.

"We contracted with Brooks Stevens to style the above-water portion of the boats. My father was well acquainted with Brooks Stevens, having worked with him 20 years earlier in connection with the Globe boats. Brooks had also done some work on styling the *Lady of the Lake*, so he understood that we wanted a classic design. He worked out the white livery on the side of the boat and also did some work on the windshield.

"We built about 25 of the 22-foot boats between 1961 and 1967. Most of them are still in use on Lake Geneva today, and many of them are still in the hands of the original purchasers. Five of the 26-foot boats were built. Each was unique in some way. One of them had twin engines and was more heavily built. Another was converted to twin engines before it was finished, and the area above the engines was covered with a

Bradley Bell, executive producer of CBS's The Bold and the Beautiful *takes time out with his wife, Colleen, and family in their Grand Craft sport runabout,* Obispo. — PHOTO BY LARRY LARKIN

Obispo

THE *Obispo*, WHICH MEANS "bishop" in Spanish, is a 21-foot 1998 Grand Craft owned by Bradley Bell, who relates: "I looked at various fiberglass boats, but in the back of my mind I really wanted a mahogany boat that still had an elegant look, that had classic lines. I did a lot of research before I found this boat. I bought all the boat magazines, such as *Classic Boating* and *Wooden Boat,* and I looked at all the web sites on the Internet.

There were only a few boatbuilders still building mahogany boats. I thought the lines of the Grand Craft were attractive and had the timeless style I was looking for. This is one of the smartest-looking mahogany boats I have seen. I also liked the utility layout. It is a great boat for water-skiing and has plenty of power. It can be used as a sport boat, and it is also the perfect boat for a young family."

Seen in front of their family home, Lucy and Karl Otzen enjoy the warm sunlight aboard their 24-foot Grand Craft,
LU-KA-LI-LE. *The name is derived from the first two letters of the family's given names: Lucy, Karl, Liza, and Lee.*

PHOTO BY R. BRUCE THOMPSON

LU-KA-LI-LE

ACCORDING TO THE BOAT'S OWNER, Karl Otzen, "I knew the Grand Craft boats had good antecedents, the lines being based on the *Gypsy*, a great performing Hackercraft that still exists on Lake Geneva. I watched Chris Smith loft the boats in the traditional style. I can still remember when the first boat was delivered. It had that wonderful new-varnish, woody smell to it. I always liked the way the boat looked, its fresh styling, and it was well built. Top speed is over 50 miles per hour, and there is no wake when you're going wide open. The boat just lays out and skims across the water."

Daughter Whitney and grandson Liam share an early morning spin past their home, Hillcroft, in Bopper, *Roger O'Neill's treasured 17-foot 1946 Chris-Craft deluxe runabout. The O'Neill flag featuring the red hand of Ulster flies from the bow staff.*

— PHOTO BY R. BRUCE THOMPSON

Chris-Craft

CHRIS-CRAFT HAD ITS ORIGIN sometime around 1870 when Christopher Columbus Smith was taught by his mother to carve wooden duck decoys. His family moved to Algonac, Michigan, just north of Detroit, and around 1884 Chris and his brother Hank started a boat livery business, renting small sailboats, rowboats, canoes and duck boats, many of which they built themselves, as well as acting as hunting guides in the Algonac area.

In 1894, the Smith brothers purchased a naphtha engine and installed it in one of their rowboats. The relative success of this installation inspired them to explore the installation of engines in more of their rowboats, and about two years later they installed a one-cylinder gasoline engine in another rowboat. It is generally agreed that this was the first installation of a gasoline engine on the Great Lakes. By 1896, they began to build small launches with canopies for their rental business.

In 1922, the company reorganized as Chris Smith and Sons, and in 1924 the name Chris-Craft began to appear on boats and other products. Boats have continued to be built under the Chris-Craft name for almost 80 years, longer than any other boat company. The Chris-Craft name has been synonymous with affordable, well-built, attractively styled boats. Many sizes and types of launches, runabouts, cruisers, and raceboats have been built over the years, and they have provided waterborne excitement and recreation for many generations of boating families.

Cream of the Kropp

Cream of the Kropp, OWNED BY Marie and Charlie Kropp, is an 18-foot Chris-Craft built in 1954 and powered by a 6-cylinder engine with triple down-draft carburetors — as is evidenced by the large chrome air-intake on the engine hatch. Charlie comments: "I loved this boat from the first time I sat in it. I was like a kid in a candy store with the instruments and engine controls. I've owned this boat for 15 years, and it still gives me a thrill to push the throttle forward and feel the boat take off, propelled by the thrust from the engine."

Marie and Charlie Kropp join seafaring forces in Cream of the Kropp, *their prized 18-foot Chris-Craft Capri.* — PHOTO BY R. BRUCE THOMPSON

Shown in front of the Hagenah Estate is Elixir, *a 24-foot 1959 Chris-Craft Sportsman owned by three brothers, Will, Phil and John Hagenah.* — PHOTO BY R. BRUCE THOMPSON

Elixir

According to the Hagenah brothers, "We had been looking for many years for a wooden boat. We bought *Elixir* in 1994, so we are the second owners. We had the boat restored by Bill Budych, who commented that it is all original. The restoration included taking everything out except the engine, a 283 Chris-Craft V-8, and redo of all the wood, trim, upholstery, flooring, and chrome. We renamed the boat *Elixir*, the magical cure for what ails you. Because of its treasured status, only a family member can be at the helm — as in Will, Phil, or John. It's the best boat we could have found, plenty of room for all of us, and reliable. Great lines, and it rides the lake beautifully."

Rare Find

"MY FATHER HAD AN OLD Gar Wood which I remember riding in as a young boy. About 15 years ago I started looking for an old woody, partly because of the memories I had of riding with my father. I found this boat over near Lake Delavan. It needed a lot of refurbishment, a new bottom, topsides restored, and the whole boat refinished. We ended up doing a complete restoration. Now the whole family enjoys going out in it, not only because of its historic aspects, but it also performs well."

Judy and Bill Pollard underway in Rare Find, *their 26-foot 1931 Chris-Craft triple-cockpit runabout.* — PHOTO BY LARRY LARKIN

A high-performance 1965 Chris-Craft Super-Sport, Water Spirit, *owned by Denise and Don Sheldon, is seen at leisure with their daughter Kayla aboard.*
— PHOTO BY R. BRUCE THOMPSON

Brian Toby, with his parents, Charleen and Dennis Toby, in his 19-foot 1966 Century Arabian powered by a 390-cubic-inch 285-horsepower Interceptor engine. The blue vinyl deck covering was characteristic of the Arabian, among the last of the wooden boats built by Century. — PHOTO BY R. BRUCE THOMPSON

*The next generation,
Cam Wrigley, takes his
grandfather's 1949 Chris-Craft,
Imp, for a spin under his father's
watchful eye. The 20-foot Riviera
has been restored as a racing
runabout with a V-6 engine.*
— PHOTO BY LARRY LARKIN

*Sailing enthusiast
Dan Ferguson observes the
races in* Legacy, *a 26-foot
1957 Chris-Craft Continental.*
— PHOTO BY R. BRUCE THOMPSON

This meticulously maintained 26-foot 1956 Chris-Craft Sea Skiff named Chuckanundah
is owned by Dianna and Charles Colman.. — PHOTO BY R. BRUCE THOMPSON

Chuckanundah

THE NAME *Chuckanundah* IS AN American Indian name that has come down through the family for several generations. It means "flowing or streaming water." Charles explains: "My father bought this Sea Skiff new in 1956. We sold it to buy a faster water-ski boat, which we had for about 20 years. When we decided to look for a better-riding boat, as luck would have it, this boat was for sale. We bought it back, fixed it up, and now receive offers to purchase it all the time. I always refuse. I won't make the same mistake twice."

Lyman

LYMAN BOAT WORKS WAS FOUNDED in Sandusky, Ohio, around 1880 by Bernard E. Lyman, a cabinetmaker who came to this country from Berlin, Germany, about 20 years earlier. Initially, he built 13-foot-long rowboats for boat liveries in a building the size of a two-car garage. Over the next 20 years, he expanded and began to build all types of boats up to 65-foot sailboats and 75-foot powerboats.

These boats became popular with experienced yachtsmen because their lapstrake construction, together with the rounded bilges, gave an easy, smooth ride. Their style and design, painted lapstrake hulls with varnished front deck and transom, and wooden-framed windshield have changed little since 1930.

Today on Lake Geneva, many of these boats are still in daily use. In a surprising number of instances, they are still owned by the families who purchased them new 50 years ago.

Abra and Jim Wilkin in Miss P.D.Q., *a 25-foot 1960 Lyman, in front of Abra's historic family home.*

— PHOTO BY R. BRUCE THOMPSON

Jim Wilkin comments about the Lyman: "The hull design and lapstrake construction give a gentle motion. The boat is very light for its size, weighing only about 60 percent of what a caravel-planked boat of the same size would weigh. They don't require much horsepower, and they slip through the water like a displacement boat, without much fuss. Up to about 15 miles per hour, there isn't anything that goes through the water as nicely. When the speed gets up near 20 or 25 miles per hour, then they begin to rise out of the water and start to plane. They are a lot of boat if you're not in a hurry."

A trio of lapstrake Lymans. Abra and Jim Wilkin, Rachel and Bill Gage, and Karl Otzen in their respective 23-foot Lymans from the 1960s — Miss P.D.Q., Shillelagh *and* Joanna. *These boats were known for their smooth, easy movement through Lake Geneva's sharp chop.*

— PHOTO BY R. BRUCE THOMPSON

This 20-foot clinker-built Lyman, named Ariel, is owned by Ellen and Bill Bentsen, frequent observers at Lake Geneva regattas. The name Ariel, an airy spirit from Shakespeare's The Tempest, *is an apt name, as Bill is an Olympic gold medal winner in sailing.*

— PHOTO BY LARRY LARKIN

1920s, a number of companies converted the engine from aircraft-type to marine applications. Because this engine bears a date of 1926, it is not the original engine for the boat but likely an effort by the boat's owner to improve the performance by installing a more powerful engine.

The hull is constructed of cypress and red cedar, both woods known for their longevity in a marine environment, with oak frames, rub rail, and interior trim. *Stardust* has been carefully restored and com-

Ulla and Bertil Brunk take time for tea in Pettersson's *attractive and cozy mahogany cabin.* — PHOTO BY R. BRUCE THOMPSON

pletely rebuilt since being purchased by Mr. Griffith. New ribs, planks, and decking have been installed. Parts necessary to rebuild the engine, including cylinder liners, were machined in Mr. Griffith's shop.

Stardust has received a number of awards, including three at the 1999 Antique Boat Show at Clayton, New York: People's Choice, Most Unique Boat, and Best Engine. As the award says, *Stardust* is a truly unique boat that has been brought back to pristine condition.

Pettersson

AN ATTRACTIVE AND UNIQUE displacement-type cruiser, the *Pettersson* was built in Sweden in 1910. The concept of the vessel came from the efforts of Carl Gustaf Pettersson, from whom the boat takes its name. Pettersson designed a series of similar engine- and sail-powered vessels to be rugged and able to stand up to the wind and wave conditions found around the Scandinavian Peninsula. This type of boat was referred to as a "Petterssonbaten."

The boat was built by Stockholm Motorbats Varv. It measures 35 feet overall length, with a 7-foot beam, a 3-foot draft, and displaces 2,500 pounds. It was originally powered by a two-cylinder Penta Model A-2 9-horsepower gasoline engine, but is currently powered by a 1968 Mercedes 55-horsepower diesel engine. The hull is constructed of Honduran mahogany over oak frames and keel.

The Pettersson's *raised freeboard forward was designed to give good protection in the rough water that can be found in the Stockholm archipelago.* — PHOTO BY R. BRUCE THOMPSON

As natives of Sweden, Bertil and Ulla Brunk had long admired these beautiful handcrafted wooden boats that graced the archipelago of Stockholm. Their dream to bring one of these boats to Lake Geneva became a reality in 1995 when Bertil was in Sweden and saw a picture of this boat in an advertisement in a Swedish boating magazine. Bertil recalls: "The boat looked interesting and was located in a boat yard in

The Pettersson, *on its marine railway cradle, being prepared for winter storage in one of the few remaining lakeshore boathouses.*
— PHOTO BY SUE LARKIN

Stockholm, not far away, so I went over to see it. When we took the covers off I thought, This is terrific! It was like love at first sight! I thought it would be a great boat for Lake Geneva, so I bought it and had it shipped over. When it arrived in the spring, I decided to restore the boat to its original condition. Since it was made of Honduran mahogany, it made the task even more difficult, because of the rarity of this fine wood. Some of the varnish was peeling, so we removed all the old varnish down to the bare wood, then scraped and sanded the wood by hand to bring out the color of the grain and applied 17 coats of varnish to complete the restoration. The beauty of the boat is a sight to behold.

"The season in Stockholm is from May to October, about the same length as the boating season here, but the climate is much colder there and the weather more severe, so the cabin and the helmsman's station is designed to provide more protection from the elements. You can sit in the cabin and enjoy drinking a little Aquavit as you are cruising along.

"It's a very nice boat to have on Lake Geneva. Ulla and I use it much the same way as they did in Sweden almost a hundred years ago, as a family boat for cruising. We love to tour the lake with our friends or go out for a quiet evening with a picnic supper for two. The charm and elegance of the *Pettersson* is one of a kind."

Allegheny

THE DESIGN OF THIS STYLISH LAUNCH, owned by Ernest and Bernice Styberg, is based on the battery-powered launches built by the Electric Launch & Navigation Company (ELCO) for the 1893 World's Fair in Chicago. These seagoing surreys-with-a-fringe-on-top launches were a popular feature, transporting over one million people a total of 200,925 miles in 66,975 trips during the Fair.

ELCO, as the company was commonly known, was founded in 1892 in Trenton, New Jersey, ostensibly to bid on the contract to supply the Columbian Exposition with 55 electric-powered launches for the Fair. ELCO was awarded the contract but did not have the manufacturing capacity in place to produce the boats. ELCO subsequently sub-contracted the manufacture of the boats to the ELCO design, some of the boats being built by the Racine Hardware Manufacturing Company located in Racine, Wisconsin.

The following excerpt is from the ELCO sales brochure: "Since their introduction, these launches have been a symbol of elegance and quality for the discerning pleasure boater. This tradition of gentility is available in the ELCO launch. On river, lake, or sound,

Slowly cruising past their 1925 home, Bernice and Ernie Styberg enjoy timeless pleasure aboard the Allegheny, *a modern rendition of the classic ELCO electric launch used at the 1893 World's Fair .* — PHOTO BY R. BRUCE THOMPSON

the smooth, quiet, gliding ride of the electric launch has given thousands of hours of pleasure to ELCO customers such as J.P. Morgan, John Jacob Astor, Henry Ford, Thomas Edison and Commodore Vanderbilt."

A number of these launches were brought to Lake Geneva following the Columbian Exposition and were used extensively around the lake. Unfortunately, none of them exist today. Their appeal lies in their charm and their ability to recapture the essence of the turn of the nineteenth century, as well as their electric power, which provides completely silent operation!

The *Allegheny* is a replica based on this 1893 design but built of modern materials, with a modern electric motor and electronic controls. The principal dimensions are virtually identical to those of the original launches built over a hundred years ago, length 30 feet, beam 6 1/2 feet, draft 2 1/4 feet, with a relative displacement of 5,000 pounds due to the propulsion batteries.

The hull of this modern version is constructed of hand-laid fiberglass saturated with polyester resin, while the hull details and trim are remarkably similar to those used originally: solid mahogany decks, white oak covering boards, sheer strake and rub rails, vertical-grain Douglas fir cabin sole, mahogany benches and ceiling. All the hardware is brass or cast-bronze polished to a high luster.

In terms of appointments and interior finish, the modern version is trimmed in oak with marine varnish finish and raised panels for an elegant appearance. The upholstery is leather with hair-stuffed cushions. The canvas canopy supported on varnished-oak bows shelters the entire accommodation area. The side curtains can be raised or lowered to enclose the passenger space during inclement weather. The boat is outfitted with a tool kit, flags, dock lines, and even a picnic basket with china, flatware, and a bottle of champagne for christening!

The motive power in today's boat is provided by a Balder 5-horsepower electric motor powered by a bank of eight storage batteries that propel the boat at 7 miles per hour. The batteries have sufficient capacity for up to 12 hours or 100 miles of cruising before a recharge is necessary. The boats meet U.S. Coast Guard requirements and have appropriate running lights and safety equipment.

Irene

IN THE 1920s, the Gould brothers built wooden rowboats and launches in their shop on Center Street in Lake Geneva. These boats were intended for the boat liveries operating out of the Riviera and were rented by tourists and used by fishing guides to take visitors out on the lake.

The *Irene* is the last survivor. Lovingly resurrected and cared for by John Buckingham, it dates from the early 1920s. It is 23 feet long with a 5-foot beam and displaces less than 1,000 pounds. The hull construction is oak ribs and stringers with cedar deck and planking.

Irene, *the last surviving 1920s Gould Brothers fishing launch, owned by Irene and John Buckingham.* — PHOTO BY R. BRUCE THOMPSON

The launch is powered by a Universal model BN Utility 4 installed in 1950, developing 15 horsepower at 1400 rpm. An assortment of bolt holes in the engine bed indicates that a number of engines have been installed over the years, the original believed to have been a one-cylinder hand-cranked engine.

"This is my favorite boat to take fishing," says John Buckingham. "You can fit four people into it comfortably and still move around, you can walk all around the engine. It doesn't go very fast, about ten miles per hour. If you push it too fast, you get water coming up over the bow because there is no flare to throw the water out. But if you're going fishing, you shouldn't be in a hurry anyhow.

"I got the boat from 'Dude' Assmann about 30 years ago. It was a wreck. He was going to take it over to the Williams Bay homecoming bonfire and throw it on the burn pile. He asked me if I wanted it, and when I said yes, he dropped it by my house.

"I liked the way it looked. I remembered them from when I was a kid. All the fishing guides had them. They used them to fish for bass, northern, and bluegills. There is some satisfaction about getting an old boat back together. I spent a year fixing it up, steam-bending new ribs and putting in new planks. It's something of a novelty, a boat as old as this one. There aren't any others from back then. This is the only one remaining on the lake. No one wants to take care of a wooden boat today, to sand it and varnish it, and you have to keep a cover on it. People don't want to go to that much trouble.

"I use it mostly for fishing. You can still catch smallmouth bass, though it's hard to find a northern that is above the 32-inch limit. Sometimes my wife and I will take a picnic supper and go out on a calm evening, watch the sunset, and fish and talk."

The Geneva, *a 50-foot former Navy personnel boat used for taking sailors from the aircraft carrier USS* Saratoga *in to shore for liberty, now takes tours on Lake Geneva.*

— PHOTO BY LARRY LARKIN

Geneva

THE *Geneva*, A 50-FOOT LAUNCH displacing 16,000 pounds, was built for the U.S. Navy in 1968 and originally assigned as a personnel boat aboard the aircraft carrier USS *Saratoga*, CV 60. It was purchased by Gage Marine in 1999 and began a new life as an excursion boat traveling along the scenic shores of Lake Geneva. The flooring was raised and the fittings and trim were upgraded. A new Caterpillar model 3208 V-8 engine replaced the original Gray Marine two-cycle diesel engine, propelling the vessel to over 10 miles per hour.

Karl Otzen's meticulously restored 1890s Whitehall rowing skiff. Note the curved ends on the sweeps and the ever so subtle mermaid signature carved into the bow.

— PHOTO BY R. BRUCE THOMPSON

Whitehall

THIS ELEGANT 18-FOOT ROWING SKIFF was built in Winter Harbor, Maine, in the 1890s to be used by the lighthouse keeper to go from Winter Harbor to the Mark Island lighthouse, located several miles off the Maine coast. It served for 90 years, until 1980, when it was purchased by Karl Otzen and brought to Lake Geneva.

The design is characteristic of skiffs and rowboats built for the severe weather conditions experienced in Maine's exposed coastal regions. The caravel planking, consisting of cedar strakes fastened with screws and rivets to oak frames, produced a sturdy, robust hull. The beauty of the hull form begins in the raised bow, with the shadow lines created by the sheer strake, carrying the eye aft along the graceful sheer to the wineglass stern. The Maine craftsmen created a work of art that is also eminently seaworthy.

The extensive restoration program took several years to complete. The hull was stripped of old paint and varnish, inside and out, using air-blasted pecan shells as an abrasive media. The interior was then restained and varnished, and the outside repainted its original white.

The sweeps were custom-made by Shaw & Tenney, specialists in Maine rowing skiffs, to match the original. They are designed for thumb-to-thumb clearance so the handles don't interfere with each other on the return stroke. The tips are inlaid with cherry so the oarsman can readily see the curve of the blade and adjust the angle of the stroke for maximum efficiency.

According to Karl, "This skiff is absolutely exquisite. It rows like a million bucks — which is about what it cost."

Old Town

THE OLD TOWN CANOE COMPANY began building canoes on the banks of the Penobscot River in Old Town, Maine, in 1898. These early canoes were modeled after birchbark canoes made by the Penobscot Indians.

This particular canoe was manufactured in 1924 and was sold through Marshall Field & Company in Chicago. It is the 17-foot OTCA model and is constructed of white cedar strips fastened to steam-bent oak frames, then covered with canvas and sealed and painted. In this top-of-the-line Class AA canoe, mahogany was used for the seats, gunwale, and thwarts, with the ends of the oak frames being secured by screws and doweled to double mahogany gunwales. The diamond-shaped heads on the brass bolts used to secure the seats are an Old Town trademark.

Every Old Town canoe has its year and serial number stamped inside the stem. The factory still maintains the original records of construction and can provide information as to the original purchaser, the construction, and the color of the canoe.

Factory records for this canoe indicate it is 17 feet long with a 35-inch beam, 13-inch depth amidships, and a weight of just over 75 pounds. Company catalogs from the period say "the flat flooring and wider beam makes this the most steady of the Old Town canoes with less loss of speed." The black-and-white dashes, reminiscent of decoration seen on older Indian canoes, are Design # 3 and were an extra-cost option.

Cam, Kristen, and Travis go exploring by the Wychwood Island Bridge in this unrestored 1924 Old Town canoe that has been in the Wrigley family for five generations.
— PHOTO BY R. BRUCE THOMPSON

The perfect picnic and family boat, Linda and John Anderson's 28-foot 1962 Lyman Islander, Vigor,
is shown in front of their south shore home. — PHOTO BY R. BRUCE THOMPSON

Vigor

OWNED BY JOHN AND LINDA ANDERSON, *Vigor* is a 28-foot Lyman sedan cruiser built in 1962 and described in the manufacturer's brochure as an Islander. It is a wide-beamed model of lapstrake construction that produces an attractive appearance and an easy ride. Powered by twin Gray Marine engines, the boat has enough power to move aggressively through the choppy wave conditions sometimes experienced on Lake Geneva.

"Because of its size, it's a great family boat and you can move around easily," reports John, "yet its arrangement lends itself to comfortable conversation. It is great for picnics and outings, for taking friends out to watch the sailboats race or to see the homes along the shoreline. And the best part is that it's a long-time Lake Geneva boat that we've given renewed life."

Lorelei

THE NAME *Lorelei* STILL HAS THE POWER to conjure visions of a mythical past. The story of the vessel begins in the early 1950s with Feadship, Inc., of Greenwich, Connecticut. Feadship represented a consortium of Dutch shipbuilders who designed and built world-class yachts using the finest European craftsmanship.

Around 1955, Feadship introduced a line of 41-foot express cruisers. Although this line was smaller than their usual designs, the vessels still had the graceful lines and were built with the same premium materials as their big sisters. Riveted steel hulls, mahogany superstructures, sleek, low deckhouses, rounded transoms, and an elegant flare to the forward sections were expensive features transposed from larger Feadships. The pilot house interior and transom were all in mahogany, the deck was planked in teak, and the window frames and hardware were hand-crafted in bronze castings and then chrome-plated.

The *Lorelei* was built by the Nicolas Witsen yard of Alkmaar, Holland, and delivered to the United States in 1954. The original name was *Dutch Maid* and the vessel spent time prior to Lake Geneva cruising the Great Lakes. In 1981, some friends told Bill Gage they had found the perfect small boat for sale in Michigan's upper peninsula. Its elegant traditional style sealed the deal.

The *Lorelei* was designed as a cruising yacht with sleeping quarters for six. In the early 1990s, Gage Marine undertook a renovation to make her more suitable for charter service and entertaining small groups on Lake Geneva. On board you will now find a mahogany saloon, a buffet serving console, and comfortable seating. This cabin, along with the teak-planked afterdeck, provides generous and elegant space for receptions of up to 16 people in classic surroundings.

The Lorelei, *a 41-foot 1954 Feadship, shows the Dutch design influence in its gracefully curving sheer.*
— PHOTO BY BILL FRANTZ

Continuing the tradition is the Quananiche, *Joan and Bob Clifford's 40-foot commuter-styled Grand Craft high-speed cruiser.*
— PHOTO BY LARRY LARKIN

Quananiche

THIS COMMUTER-STYLED HIGH-SPEED cruiser by Grand Craft of Holland, Michigan, was built for Robert Clifford. The design is based on a John Alden-designed commuter circa 1930, a style popular particularly in the Long Island region of New York. It combines classic form with modern materials.

Quananiche takes its name from the land-locked salmon. With a length of 40 feet, a 12-foot beam, and displacing 18,000 pounds, it is one of the largest wooden cruisers to be built in the United States in recent years. Construction uses a system of thin mahogany strips saturated with epoxy resin placed against each other with alternate layers crisscrossing. When the resin cures, the hull becomes a homogenous structure that has great strength.

The Quananiche is powered by twin V-8 360-horsepower Peninsular Diesel engines equipped with turbo-chargers. The engines have been specially detailed, with machined aluminum components replacing steel stampings to prevent rust and corrosion, and the accessories have been chrome-plated and polished. With these engines the boat can cruise slowly yet have the power for high-speed performance. Two side thrusters will provide maneuverability for docking. The boat's top speed is expected to be in excess of 40 miles per hour.

Robert Clifford: "A few years ago we purchased a summer home that Judge Sears had built around the turn of the century. The judge had a steamboat called the Quananiche for cruising on Lake Geneva that fit the lifestyle of the period. It seemed to make sense to use the same name. The era of steamboats has passed now, but the way they were used — as a means of enjoying the lake — is still with us.

"I wanted a classic launch reminiscent of the turn-of-the-century steam-powered launches that were unique to Lake Geneva, but none of them exist anymore, so I commissioned Grand Craft to build this one for me. This is really a unique boat. It can be used as an elegant water limousine for transportation around the lake, or for family cruising, and it will have a full galley aboard, so it can be easily used for entertaining.

"We went to Grand Craft because they were familiar with Lake Geneva and understood the way we intended to use the boat. I gave them a vision; they gave me a concept. We wanted an open bow with seating, a midship cabin with the captain's station, galley, and serving areas, and we wanted an afterdeck for dining and congregating. A wooden canopy provides good protection from inclement weather."

"Bob wanted the best of everything," said interior designer Jessica Lagrange. Exquisite details such as delicate antique gold roping around the nickel plated door handles, engraved glassware, and polished brass Turk's-head knots on the drawer pulls adorn the cabin interior. Custom-made wicker furniture by Bielecky Brothers of New York upholstered with hand-printed Vennison fabrics from London is built into the cabin and afterdeck.

On a balmy summer evening, sister ships Ada E *and* Normandie *cruise tranquilly, silhouetted by the aurorean sunset.* — PHOTO BY R. BRUCE THOMPSON

Chapter 4

THE FAMED
LAKE GENEVA YACHTS

At the turn of the nineteenth century, the steam yacht proved to be the ideal means of conveyance for the waterborne explorer to visit the many enchanting bays and points along the Lake Geneva shoreline. The steam yacht captured the very essence of the era. These impressive yachts are a link to our heritage, to that age past when the quiet elegance of Lake Geneva's golden age evolved and flourished.

This particular style of yacht or day cruiser, characterized by the long, open deck forward, deckhouse amidships, and small afterdeck, is unique to Lake Geneva and is not found in any other part of the country. These boats were initially developed and built locally, the first ones being built on the shores of Lake Geneva from trees quartered and sawn in mills along the White River. They were intended to meet the need for functional transportation between the villages around the lake and to the summer homes and estates that were beginning to be established along the lakeshore. Their era began in 1872, about the time the Chicago & North Western Railroad linking Chicago and Lake Geneva was completed, and peaked around 1910. With the growing popularity of the automobile and completion of paved roads around the lake, the need for these craft declined, with the last being launched in 1913.

Although the early boats that were built locally were somewhat utilitarian, it wasn't long before more elegant ones were being built in Racine and Chicago and, toward the end of the era, in New York City. These yachts were superb models of marine architecture. Smooth, graceful lines complemented their tasteful proportions. Brass hardware and accessories were polished to a mirror finish, while bleached-white holystoned decks contrasted with the rich mahogany woodwork finished with glistening varnish. A uniformed captain in gold braid and his solicitous crew saw to the comfort of guests.

The fact that five of these historically significant vessels — *Matriark*, *Ada E*, *Polaris*, *Hathor*, and *Normandie* — still exist in substantially their original form is remarkable. Their owners' sense of stewardship and commitment to preserve them in their original configuration and protect their design integrity is commendable.

The restorations and new construction of the past few years indicate that there is still considerable interest in continuing Lake Geneva's unique heritage. The reconstructed *Louise* and the new tugboat-styled yacht *Benjamin F. Bates* are interesting boats in their own right and part of the evolving Lake Geneva scene.

Late afternoon sunlight brightens Matriark's *cabin, highlighting the warm glow of the mahogany buffet.*
— PHOTO BY R. BRUCE THOMPSON

Matriark

ORIGINALLY CHRISTENED THE *Passaic*, the *Matriark* was built by the Racine Boat Manufacturing Company in 1899 especially for Richard T. Crane, founder of the Crane Plumbing Company. The name came from the town of Passaic, New Jersey, where the Crane family first established residence in the United States before moving to Chicago. The vessel was originally painted white with an orange-and-black smokestack that captured the colors of the Crane Company.

The following is taken from the Racine Boat Manufacturing Company catalog dated 1904:

The *Passaic* was built by us for Mr. R. T. Crane in 1899 for use at his summer home on Lake Geneva. Her construction is entirely of steel, all double riveted with water tight athwartship bulkheads, coal bunkers, white pine deck laid fore and aft in narrow strips, caulked and filled with marine glue, mahogany railings supported on polished turned brass stanchions with rope netting. The deck house is built of white mahogany throughout and presents a very handsome appearance. The toilet room has onyx wash basin and a flush closet operated by a pump and air compressor in the engine room. The coat room is opposite with necessary conveniences. Main cabin has a very handsome buffet and divan, upholstered seat and back in leather. All windows are plate glass and are arranged to drop into pockets. A rack and pinion steering gear is installed with a polished brass steering stand and mahogany steering wheel. A compass and binnacle is mounted on top of the steering sand with bell pulls on the side. The machinery consists of compound engine and Scotch Marine Boiler developing 125 horsepower driving the yacht about 14 miles per hour. The price on this yacht would range from $12,000 to $14,000 depending on specifications.

The *Passaic* was designed by naval architect George Warrington shortly before he was appointed Under-Secretary of Commerce by Theodore Roosevelt. It was the last boat he designed, and probably the most elegant, in his long career as a naval architect before he left for Washington, D.C. Further, it was built by the Racine Boat Manufacturing Company at a time when that company was the premier yacht builder in this part of the country. All these attributes contributed to the outstanding appearance and quality of this yacht.

Three generations of the Gage family enjoy a picnic supper on the Matriark*'s after deck.*
— PHOTO BY R. BRUCE THOMPSON

At 87 feet in length, with a 13-foot beam, 5-foot draft, and displacement of nearly 40 tons, it is by any measure the largest privately-owned boat on the lake, which in itself would be noteworthy. But this particular yacht is more than the sum of its specifications. With its gracefully curved clipper bow, fitted with a bowsprit in the style of the old clipper ships, to its elliptically curved stern, the sheer has a smooth, powerful line from bow to stern. The towering masts and tall smokestack add a lofty majesty. From any point of view, the subtle continuing change in curvature of the lines of the hull create a harmonious design.

At the time this vessel was built, there was a transition in naval architecture from sailing vessels to engine-powered ships. As a result, the external appearance of many vessels from this period still carried design elements held over from the clipper ship era, such as tall masts, clipper bow, and fantail stern, while the source of motive power changed to steam and, a short time later, to petroleum-fueled internal combustion engines. A few years later, vessels of this type would lose the graceful classic lines of the clipper ship era, with the

*Silhouetted against a cloudless blue sky, the Matriark's twin masts
combine with its clipper bow and graceful sheer to create a harmony of design.* — PHOTO BY LARRY LARKIN

bow becoming a straight-lined vertical or plumb bow and the fantail and rounded stern sections becoming flat transoms. This yacht remains as a wonderful example of the classic clipper-ship style before it merged into the new style of engine-driven vessels.

The boat was last used by the Crane family in the summer of 1930 when it was put back in commission especially for the Crane Company's 75th anniversary celebration. In 1933, the boat was sold to the Delavan Lake Excursion Company, renamed the *Clipper*, and moved to Lake Delavan. However, the boat had difficulty navigating around the shallow regions of the lake, and the anticipated excursion business never developed on that lake. In 1945, after World War II, the boat was moved back to Lake Geneva, where it sat derelict before being saved from an ignominious demise.

Maggie Gage enjoys a quiet moment on the Matriark's *after deck.*
— PHOTO BY R. BRUCE THOMPSON

In 1949, the boat was purchased by Russell Gage. Russ told his 13-year-old son, Bill, to find an old boat they could fix up as a father-son project. Bill trolled the shores of the lake in his fishing skiff, powered by an 8-horsepower outboard, in search of a fixer-upper. Out of everything he saw, the boat that caught his eye was this old lake steamer moored to a buoy in Williams Bay. When Bill pointed the boat out to Russ

for the first time, Russ nearly fell out of the boat. Russ recalls: "It was in terrible shape — gray woodwork, rotten decks, paint flaking off. There was no engine, and the reduction gear had been installed in such a way that the engine would have needed to be run in reverse to get the boat to go forward. I don't know how they ever ran it that way. But the hull was in reasonably good shape and you couldn't hide the beauty of the lines. There was something special about the boat."

A week later, in fact on Russ's birthday, the paperwork was done and he came home and told his wife to take a good look at him because it had taken all those years to get as crazy as he was.

That fall and winter the boat went through a complete restoration. A new Kermath Sea Farer Special 225-horsepower engine was installed, along with a new canopy and deck, and portions of the cabin were replaced. Rechristened *Matriark*, the boat was launched in 1950.

By the early 1980s, the *Matriark* was showing her age, the boat had gone over 30 years since her only major renovation, and a difficult decision was made to take her out of the water and go through the boat, completely replacing or rebuilding all the necessary parts. Approximately 30 percent of the steel hull plating was replaced, the cabin was completely replaced, and the washroom was returned to its original location. A new canopy was constructed of aluminum, and the deck replaced. All the mechanical equipment was installed, which included a new Caterpillar 3208 diesel engine and an Onan 8-kilowatt generator.

Many years ago, while in Holland, Michigan, Bill Gage had been impressed by the beauty of a cutter-rigged sailboat, which had a dark blue hull with a high-gloss finish and a varnished deckhouse. Bill thought that treatment of the hull, along with the polished brass hardware created a very attractive combination. When the *Matriark* was restored, Bill wanted to incorporate this style in the restored *Matriark*.

In order to accomplish a high-gloss finish on the hull, particularly with a dark color, all of the unevenness of rivet heads, lapped plate seams and weld lines had to be faired from bow to stern. Epoxy compounds were used to fill any low spots, and the entire hull was sanded to a perfectly smooth surface. A navy blue Awl-Grip enamel was applied to the hull sides, resulting in a glistening, porcelain-like finish. The Philippine mahogany cabin was stained to enhance the grain of the wood, and multiple coats of varnish were applied

Owner Bill Gage at the helm of the 100-year-old Matriark.
— PHOTO BY R. BRUCE THOMPSON

to create a high-gloss finish. A deep-throated Kahlenberg whistle, reminiscent of the steamboat era, was also added.

The sense of stewardship has always run strong for Bill, but no more so than with the *Matriark*: "We have been fortunate to be in a position to bring together skilled craftsmen and have a business that has allowed us to restore a living part of Lake Geneva history. The *Matriark* has always been a place, an environment, where all the generations can be together; it is very much about family. At the end of the night, everyone pitches in and either cleans dishes, puts on the nightlines or helps cover the boat. I have wonderful memories of evenings I spent with friends of my parents and relatives as I grew up, and now as we are grandparents I know that future generations will have that same opportunity."

Still owned by the Gage family, it is a historically important yacht as well as a familiar sight on Lake Geneva. Its size, unique clipper bow, tall masts, and signature navy blue hull attracts every admiring eye. The *Matriark* is held in high regard by all who are privileged to witness this elegant vessel's graceful movement through the waters of Lake Geneva.

The 70-foot 1911 Ada E *is owned by William Wrigley, Jr., fourth-generation descendant of the original owner.*
— PHOTO BY R. BRUCE THOMPSON

Ada E

OF ALL THE EARLY DAY CRUISERS, launches, steam and motor yachts on Lake Geneva, the *Ada E* occupies a unique place, in that it has always been owned by the same family. Indeed, each generation has recognized that this yacht is historically important and taken their ownership more as a stewardship of a prized asset. The

Ada E has been passed down through four generations in the Wrigley family, each, in turn, respecting the historical significance and family traditions and maintaining the yacht in first-class condition. It is owned today by William Wrigley, Jr., great-grandson of the original builder.

The *Ada E* was commissioned in 1911 by William Wrigley, Jr., founder of the William Wrigley Company. The vessel was designed by Charles L. Seabury and built by the Gas Engine and Power Company, located on City Island in Morris Heights, New York City. This was the first time that a New York company had been retained to build one of these yachts. Since 1890, virtually all had been built in Racine, Wisconsin. However, after the Racine Boat Manufacturing Company burned in 1903, there were no readily available local sources for construction of these vessels.

The *Ada E* was named for Mr. Wrigley's wife, a practice that became a Wrigley family tradition. The yacht is best described by a contemporary newspaper article reporting on the construction of the yacht:

Mr. Wrigley, Jr's. new power yacht, the *Ada E*, for day service on Western Waters

Mr. William Wrigley, Jr., of Chicago is having built at the works of the Gas Engine and Power Company and Charles L. Seabury & Co., of Morris Heights, N.Y., a large cruising power yacht for day service on Lake Geneva, Wisconsin. The yacht will be named the *Ada E*, and was designed by Seabury in accordance with Mr. Wrigley's wishes.

The yacht will be 70 feet over all, 13 feet beam and 4 feet draft. The hull is of steel, and the construction will be of the most approved and up to date character. The deck, both forward and aft, is spacious and unobstructed, affording the pleasantest of views.

The cabin is commodious and will contain a buffet and the additional regulation equipment for a craft of this size and service. The decks will be laid with white pine, in yacht style, and the joiner work throughout the vessel will be of mahogany. Electricity will be used in lighting the craft, and all the furnishings have been selected with the usual care and will be arranged in harmonious colors.

The motive power of the *Ada E* will consist of two 4-cylinder, (6 x 8 inches) 4-cycle Speedway engines developing from 50 to 60 horsepower each, which will insure the guaranteed speed of 13 miles per hour. The engines will be controlled from the steering wheel, so that one man may handle the yacht, if necessary.

The vessel will be ready for delivery at any time in the early spring desired by her owner. The intention is to send the *Ada E* from New York to Chicago by way of the canals and lakes, and then transport the vessel by rail to Fontana, Wisconsin [sic], where she will be placed in Lake Geneva.

There are many cruising day boats on Lake Geneva, but they are equipped with steam power, so that the *Ada E*, with its internal combustion engines, may be regarded as a novelty and prove both attractive and popular.

The newspaper article accurately portrayed the yacht as the first gasoline-powered day cruiser on the lake, and it had twin engines at that. These engines were massive four-cylinder engines with a displacement of 1,060 cubic inches. Because electric starters were still some years in the future, the engines were turned over by hand, using a 3-foot lever with a ratchet that fit around the crankshaft. The starting process was elaborate and involved squirting gasoline into a primer cup, then turning the engine over with the starting bar to compress the gasoline vapor in the cylinders, then causing a spark to occur, which ignited the gasoline vapor and air mixture at the proper time. According to Philip Wrigley, "They would occasionally start the first time, but to be sure, the captain and motor mechanic would allow two hours to get the engines running."

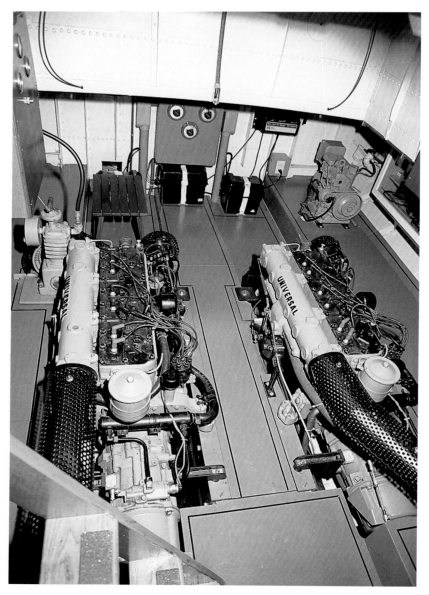

The Ada E's spotless engine room, with twin Universal
6-cylinder engines, is a testament to John Buckingham's
meticulous attention to detail.

— PHOTO BY R. BRUCE THOMPSON

The symmetrical layout of the instruments and engine
controls at the steering station as seen from the helmsman's
station on the Ada E's forward deck.

— PHOTO BY R. BRUCE THOMPSON

Although of lighter construction than the earlier Racine Boat Company boats, the hull nonetheless possessed fine lines and was constructed with the craftsmanship typical of other yachts built in the east. Again, according to Philip Wrigley, "An interesting fact about the *Ada E's* steel hull is that it was built before the days of welding so the hull plates are riveted together but no rivets show on the outside. All the rivets used were flatheaded and then countersunk to make the hull perfectly smooth.

"When the *Ada E* was shipped to Lake Geneva from New York, she came through the New York State Barge Canal and the Great Lakes under her own power. In Kenosha, they got a house-moving outfit to pull her out of the water and load her on a three flatcars, resting on one and hanging out over the other two. That is when their troubles really started. Because of the 13-foot beam, they had to take down the corner of a brick building and then rebuild it after the boat was past. Since they had contracted to deliver the boat to Lake Geneva for a flat price, they ended up in the red."

The cabin was exceptionally roomy and constructed of recessed Honduran mahogany panels. On either side of the cabin, tufted red leather cushions were placed on built-in benches that could serve as

Built-in benches flank the sides of the Ada E's *stately cabin.*
— PHOTO BY R. BRUCE THOMPSON

bunks. Lace curtains covered the windows. A drop-side table was specially built and installed in the cabin for dining. It had special bolts that screwed into deck plates to anchor it in place. The deck was laid with narrow strips of white pine with caulked white seams. Inside the cabin, the cabin sole was covered wall to wall with a dark blue carpet. Around the deck ran a polished brass handrail, since replaced with stainless steel of the same dimensions.

The *Ada E* has been carefully preserved and well maintained, and is in nearly the same condition it was in 90 years ago. The only significant changes are new engines that were installed on two occasions over the lifetime of the vessel, replacement of some brass and steel parts with stainless steel, and the replacement of the original manila lines with nylon. The materials used in maintenance and refurbishment from time to time have been, so far as possible, the same as the original materials. For example, when the deck was replaced a few years ago, the same clear white pine that had been used in the original deck was located, carefully seasoned, painstakingly cut to the same size, and laid in exactly the same manner to ensure authenticity.

Normandie

The *Normandie* was built in 1913 for Norman Harris, founder of the Harris Bank in Chicago. According to myth, the name is derived from the principal maritime province of France, using the Old French spelling, but it is also a variant of the name of one of Mr. Harris's sons, Norman D. Harris. The vessel was designed by Charles L. Seabury and built by the Gas Engine and Power Company, City Island, New York City, the company later becoming Consolidated Shipbuilding Company .

The *Normandie* is 63 feet long with an 11-foot beam. Its hull is constructed of one-inch-thick cypress planking fastened with copper clinch rivets to white oak frames. The original engine was a massive 6-cylinder Speedway engine with each cylinder measuring 6-inch bore by 7-inch stroke, giving 1,200 cubic inches of displacement. The engine was a work of art itself, with polished brass piping, bronze castings, and painted in a glossy two-tone gray color.

There is no doubt that Mr. Harris was very involved in the design of the boat, because the

The genteel essence of the Normandie *lives on as an afternoon tea is served. A sunbeam highlights a handcarved seashell on the built-in mahogany buffet.*

— PHOTO BY R. BRUCE THOMPSON

Members of the Lake Geneva Chapter of the Chicago Lyric Opera Guild arrive for a program at the Richard Driehaus estate, former home of Norman Harris, the original owner of the Normandie. — PHOTO BY R. BRUCE THOMPSON

Pillaging pirates and marauding miscreants aboard the Normandie *are repelled by seasoned cannoniers Fred Geldermann and Cully Pillman. The cannon, named* Admiral Boom, *is modelled after the historic British 6-pounder used aboard Admiral Nelson's flagship and adopted by the Americans during the Revolutionary War.*

— PHOTO BY R. BRUCE THOMPSON

Normandie was the most elegantly appointed of all the Lake Geneva yachts. The cabin is made from Honduran mahogany, inside and out, with a very fine, uniform grain. The inside of the cabin is done with recessed panels surrounded by delicately detailed moldings. Elegant turnings were used in the trim, and aquatic images such as dolphins and seashells were carved in relief to accent the cabin paneling. The faucets and plumbing fixtures were nickel-plated and the light fixtures gold-plated. It was one of the first boats to be equipped with hot and cold water in the galley and head. Fine china and crystal were engraved with the yacht's name. The scrollwork at the bow was handcarved into the hull with gold leaf applied to the recesses.

The *Normandie* was the last Lake Geneva day cruisers to be built. As automotive transportation became reliable and widespread, the need for this type of boat diminished. The few that remain today are historically important, not only because they represent an evolutionary period in marine architecture, but also because they provide a link to that elegant earlier age of boating on Lake Geneva.

Sitting on the forward deck, Augie, Avery, Bradley, and Cricket Geldermann muster for a game of cards on the Normandie'*s nameplate.* — PHOTO BY R. BRUCE THOMPSON

ABOVE:
*Placed in front of the helm,
a bench with a handcarved
dolphin highlights the
Normandie's front deck.*

AT LEFT:
*Eliptical fantail displays her
name in vintage style*

AT RIGHT:
*The Normandie's after deck is
a favorite quarter for enjoying
a cruise or sunbathing.*

— PHOTOS BY R. BRUCE THOMPSON

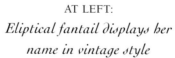

Hathor

THE *Hathor* WAS BUILT BY the Racine Boat Manufacturing Company in 1898 for Martin A. Ryerson and was one of a group of three virtually identical boats built for Lake Geneva residents. Hathor was the Egyptian goddess of love and joy and it was also the name of the Nile River barge that the Ryersons stayed aboard when they honeymooned in Egypt.

The Racine Boat Manufacturing Company's 1902 catalog describes these craft:

> This group of steam yachts are our own creation being built for pleasure purposes on Lake Geneva. They are 73 feet overall; 12-foot beam and 4-foot draft; constructed entirely of steel with five water-tight compartments. The machinery consists of a Racine water tube boiler and one of our 6, 10, & 16 x 9-inch stroke triple expansion engines developing 200 indicated horsepower and giving a speed of fifteen miles per hour. Mahogany finish throughout; electric lights and modern conveniences. Very beautiful, speedy, safe and economical craft that will meet the views of the most fastidious in every particular. Price $13,500.00.

Current oners Owen and Bonnie Deutsch relax on the shaded veranda of the former Ryerson estate as the Hathor basks in its own reflection, anchored as it would have been 100 years earlier.

— PHOTOS BY ???

Martin Ryerson commissioned the *Hathor*. He was the scion to a Michigan lumber fortune. He had attended schools in Paris, France, and Geneva, Switzerland, before coming to Chicago around 1860 and marrying Carrie Hutchinson. In a short time, he became a well-known Chicago civic leader and major benefactor to many of the city's finest institutions. Contemporary newspaper accounts describe Ryerson as a distinguished philanthropist and art connoisseur. He was president of the University of Chicago for over 30 years, a trustee of the Field Museum, a founder of the Art Institute, and a director of the Northern Trust Company. He was known for his discriminating taste in art and purchased many works directly from artists such as Renoir, Monet, Cezanne, and Gauguin. He later donated to these paintings to the Art Institute, thus forming the nucleus of the museum's extensive French Impressionist collection.

The Ryerson estate, currently owned by Owen and Bonnie Deutsch, was magnificent at its peak, with over 1,200 feet of lake frontage and 100 acres of prime lakeshore property on the north shore just east of the

The Hathor, *built in 1898 by Martin Ryerson, nestles in front of the Ryerson estate.*
It was moored in this cove 100 years earlier. On the front deck of the Hathor *are Bonnie and Owen Deutsch, current*
owners of the Ryerson estate, with owner Bill Sills at the wheel in a period captain's uniform. — PHOTO BY LARRY LARKIN

narrows. During the summer months, 20 employees lived on the grounds, including 6 maids, a butler, a houseman, a chauffeur, a foreman for the estate, and 8 gardeners. Of course, there was also the captain and engineer to care for and operate the 73-foot steam yacht.

The vessel's design is characterized by a vertical bow, small day cabin amidships, and a small transomed stern. At the time the boat was built, the design was a departure from earlier vessels, which still showed elements from sailing ships in their hull form. It represented a trend toward hulls designed especially for steam power, without the decorative sailboat trappings generally found on steam-powered cruising yachts of the period.

The steamer was heavily built, with 3/16-inch-thick steel hull plating riveted to the frames. It displaced close to 40 tons when fully loaded with coal and with the boilers full in operating condition. The engine room was maintained in spotless condition, and the engine was so well adjusted and lubricated that it would turn over almost noiselessly with as little as 15 pounds of steam pressure.

The *Hathor's* cabin measures 14 feet long and was richly furnished in the manner of a library, with recessed mahogany paneling and an abundance of handcarved ornamentation. Newspaper accounts from 1898 describe the *Hathor's* cabin as a "glory of mahogany with brass and silver fittings and with great crimson silk cushions bearing the name Hathor that was subtly woven into the fabric." A buffet table was often set up for entertaining in the cabin, with an elaborate silver service and music provided by a Victrola.

The *Hathor* is currently owned by William H. Sills III and is again a frequent sight on the lake. "I always loved the unique Geneva Lake steam yachts," says Bill. "As a small boy, the steamers were the major daily excitement on the lake. I remember the *Tula* circling around, picking up passengers in the early morning and taking them to the train station in Williams Bay, where they would board the train for the trip to Chicago.

"I have the *Hathor* because of a combination of being very lucky and very persistent. We enjoy the sunset cruises with friends, weekend cruising with light luncheons, and supper cruises. The *Hathor* is also frequently used as a guest boat at yacht club regattas, and traditionally follows the Sheridan Trophy race each Labor Day weekend.

"As a longtime National Sea Scout officer, I have had many members of the Girl Scouts, including Brownies, Cadets, Junior and Mariner Scouts aboard, as well as Cub Scouts, Boy Scouts and Sea Scouts — sometimes as many as 400 during a season. We have also had aboard many local Scout volunteers and Scout professionals for appreciation cruises.

"The steamer has always represented excitement, fun, and a sense of freedom. One of the best parts of my life has been the good fortune to be able to bring some of the joy I have felt about these Geneva Lake steamboats to so many others aboard *Hathor*."

Built in 1898 by the Racine Boat Company for Otto Young, the Polaris *cruises past its former home, Younglands, seen off the bow.* — PHOTO BY LARRY LARKIN

Polaris

THE *Polaris* WAS ANOTHER OF the three virtually identical boats built by the Racine Boat Manufacturing Company in 1898. It measures 73 feet long and has a 12-foot beam. It can be easily identified by the five window panels in the white cabin. The 1902 Racine Boat Company catalog describes the cabin as being "neatly finished in white enamel."

Originally named *Olivette,* the vessel was built for Otto Young, a real estate magnate from Chicago who also founded the Fair Store. Otto Young is best known today, around Lake Geneva, as the builder of the Italianate villa, or *palazzo,* that he called Younglands but which is now commonly known as Stone Manor.

The *Polaris* was purchased in the early 1940s by the Wisconsin Transportation Company, which later became Gage Marine. Because of the fine condition of the yacht, it was not placed on scheduled service but used principally for charters and private parties.

Cheryl and Harold Friestad at the wheel of the Polaris. *As General Manager of the Geneva Lake Cruise Line, Harold was largely responsible for the restoration of the* Polaris.
— PHOTO BY LARRY LARKIN

By the early 1970s, a thorough renovation was deemed necessary. Gage Marine repowered the boat, this time with a Caterpillar 3208 V-8 diesel engine. The canopy was repaired, the hull plating was inspected and replaced as necessary. The deck was replaced with clear Northern white pine, portions of the paneled saloon were painstakingly restored, and a mahogany enclosure for the wheel house was added. Almost all of the original 1898 brass fittings remained intact and were repolished to a glistening appearance. With the open center portion of its deck located where

the steam-engine room used to be, and a bar and head in the saloon, the *Polaris* is still elegantly appointed.

The *Polaris* has undergone a number of upgrades and is in excellent condition. It is a unique boat with a hundred-year-old character, a link between nineteenth and twenty-first centuries.

The elegant restored cabin of the Polaris *offers guests a step back to an earlier era.* — PHOTO BY LARRY LARKIN

The rush of wet steam and the whistle's distinctive resonant bellow announcing the arrival of the Louise *can be heard for miles.* — PHOTO BY R. BRUCE THOMPSON

Louise

THE LARGEST PROPELLER-DRIVEN, steam-powered passenger boat in the Midwest today, the *Louise* is a true survivor. It was built in 1902 by the Racine Boat Manufacturing Company for John J. Mitchell, a well-known banker and a founder of the Continental Illinois National Bank and Trust Company in Chicago. The yacht was christened *Louise* in honor of Mitchell's wife and was used frequently by the Mitchells for entertaining guests and visiting friends around the lake.

The *Louise* is 75 feet long, and its 15-foot beam was the widest of any of the boats from the steamboat era. This extra width allowed a walkway around each side of the cabin so that the after deck was accessible without going through the cabin.

There can be no doubt that the *Louise* was a very fine and well-kept yacht from the outset. Anecdotes by those who were familiar with the yacht when it was operated by the Mitchells mention oriental carpets on the deck, wicker furniture, silver service for refreshments in the cabin, all epitomizing elegance.

The engine room was absolutely immaculate. Brass steam gauges, prominently placed and highly polished, monitored the engine performance. The electrical meters and controls for the steam-driven generator were mounted on a polished marble control panel. The round brass covers on each of the three cylinders on the Racine triple-expansion steam engine were also polished to a mirror finish, as were the

Built by the Racine Boat
Company in 1902 for John
Mitchell, Louise *is the only
large steamboat operating
in the Midwest.*

— PHOTO BY R. BRUCE THOMPSON

The spacious cabin of the Louise *has
ample room to serve a buffet for 50 people.*

— PHOTO BY R. BRUCE THOMPSON

levers and valves that controlled the engine. The aft end of the horizontal fire-tube coal-fired boiler was fitted with a large, round, polished brass cover on the boiler face, engraved with the yacht's name in script: "*Steam Yacht Louise.*"

Following the Mitchells' tragic death in a car accident, the *Louise* was purchased from the Mitchell estate by the Wisconsin Transportation Company, the principal excursion boat company operating on Lake Geneva at that time. The wicker furniture, oriental carpet and fine appointments were removed and replaced with canvas deck chairs and accessories more suitable for a commercial vessel. The *Louise* was operated commercially for over 40 years. In 1960, the cabin was removed and the name changed to the *City of Lake Geneva* for a brief period.

By 1970, a succession of gasoline engines had worn out and the hull plating had deteriorated and needed repair or replacement. Because the vessel had seemingly reached the end of its life, it was stripped of its superstructure, and the bare hull was hauled overland to the Gage Marine storage building located about a mile west of Williams Bay.

Engineer James Markel operates the forward/reverse valve linkage and throttle of the Louise's *steam engine.*

— PHOTO BY R. BRUCE THOMPSON

Bill Gage shared a lifelong interest in steam with his father, Russell, an interest extending back to Bill's grandfather, who owned a steam threshing rig and obtained a patent on a force-feed lubricator for steam engines. Although they had talked about building a steamboat for many years, the restoration of the *Louise* was Bill's vision. It would take nearly a decade and many thousands of hours of work by dedicated and highly skilled craftsmen, experts in welding, woodworking, and engine technicians, to complete the project. It would not have become a reality without Bill's vision and determination, both so instrumental in the conception and completion of the restoration project.

The original triple-expansion engine had long since been sold for scrap, and engines of this type seemingly did not exist anymore. Undaunted, Bill Gage went to England and fortuitously discovered a steam engine of appropriate size and horsepower advertised in a newsletter published by the Steamboat Association of Great Britain. The engine was described as a two-cylinder compound with principal cylinder dimensions of "8 & 16 X 8," able to produce over 120 horsepower at a speed of 200 rpm.

The steam engine has a unique history of its own. It was manufactured in 1926 by Plenty & Son, of Newbury, England, a builder of steam engines since 1790. The Plenty engine originally powered a 52-foot British Admiralty harbor launch that had recently plied the waters of the Thames River. This launch was used to transport soldiers from France to England during the evacuation at Dunkirk in 1940, making 17 trips back and forth across the Channel. With the purchase of the engine, the opportunity for the restoration of the *Louise* as a steamboat became a reality.

The engine was shipped to the United States, then sent to Norman Sandley, a well-known builder of small steam engines and narrow-gauge steam locomotives, located at Wisconsin Dells. Over a four-year period, the engine was completely disassembled, cleaned, inspected, and carefully rebuilt. Any part showing wear or deterioration was replaced by a new handmade part. The lagging wood strips that provided insulation around the cylinders were replaced with new osage orange strips that were subsequently varnished.

Meanwhile, back at the Gage Marine boatyard, work was commencing to rebuild the *Louise's* hull. Bernie Hackbarth, who had previously overseen

Captain Mark McGinn has crewed on the Louise *for the past 20 years.*
— PHOTO BY R. BRUCE THOMPSON

construction of the *Belle of the Lake*, was responsible for the mechanical restoration. He possessed a rare combination of technical expertise and managerial skill and was largely responsible for the quality of the restoration.

A careful inspection of the hull revealed that virtually all the plating would have to be replaced, along with many of the frames and deck beams. This alone required over two years of work. The old plating was removed section by section by cutting off the rivet heads and driving out the rivets. Using the old hull plates as patterns, new 3/16-inch-thick steel plates were cut, formed to the proper curvature, and welded into place. Forming the hull plates was especially difficult because most of them had complex curves where they were curved in two directions. In some cases, this necessitated stretching the metal so that the plates would lie snugly against the frames.

Finally, after eight years of reconstruction, the boat was launched toward the end of the 1978 season. Today, almost 25 years later, the *Louise* is more frequently used and enjoyed by more people than at any previous time in its life. The centennial of her original completion and launch will be celebrated in 2002.

Benjamin F. Bates

ALBEN F. (PETER) BATES, JR.'S lifelong association with Lake Geneva began in the 1930s when he was a young boy spending summers at the family cottage in Rainbow Bay near Fontana. His lifelong fascination with boats, especially interesting and unusual boats, dates from his earliest years: "I remember around 1935 seeing the *Doreen* come in to the fuel pier in Fontana to take on coal. At that time, the *Doreen* was the most beautiful boat on the lake. With its graceful clipper bow and long stern overhang leading back to the transom, it was really something! The size of the boat was overwhelming, and everything shined and glistened in the sunlight. It was steam-powered at the time, one of the last, and was that engine beautiful! It didn't make a sound, and it ran so smoothly that you couldn't tell it was running. From that time on, I was fascinated with boats in general and steam engines in particular."

As a young man, Peter avidly perused the design sections of yachting magazines. He would paste pictures and drawings of interesting boats on the walls of his home to look at from different perspectives. One time he sent his father a picture of a two-masted cruising sailboat with the plaintive question: "Ask yourself why you're living if not to own a boat like this." He built model boats powered by gasoline

engines. He read books by and about major designers such as Herreshoff, Alden, and numerous others, and was an avid reader of the design sections of various nautical magazines.

In the Second World War, Peter was in the Army, stationed for three years on Espiritu Santo, in the New Hebrides Islands. This was the site of a large replenishment base for the Navy, as well as the first U.S. airstrip

Underway, the Bates family enjoys an evening dinner cruise on the after deck.

— PHOTO BY R. BRUCE THOMPSON

Benjamin F. Bates, a tugboat-styled yacht built in 1992 by Palmer Johnson for Alben F. Bates, Jr.
— PHOTO BY R. BRUCE THOMPSON

in the South Pacific and the point of origin for B-17 raids on Guadalcanal. Peter saw many different types of watercraft during his tour of duty and had ample opportunity to reflect on the more subtle aspects of ship design. In 1946, shortly after his return to civilian life, one of his first purchases was an 18-foot surplus Navy personnel boat that was perfect for picnics and outings to watch sailboat races.

The culmination of his lifelong boat-acquisition plan is the *Benjamin F. Bates*, a tugboat-styled yacht 63 feet long with a 20-foot beam, displacing 80,000

pounds. It was built in 1991 by Palmer Johnson in Sturgeon Bay, Wisconsin.

The *Benjamin F. Bates* takes its name from Peter Bates's great-great-grandfather, a whaling ship captain who sailed out of Massachusetts in the early 1770s. During the Revolutionary War, his ship was requisitioned by General George Washington to ferry troops and was subsequently sunk in the war effort. The Continental Congress later compensated Benjamin Bates with a land grant of 10,000 acres near present-day Painesville, Ohio, in what was then known as the

ABOVE: *The inviting saloon aboard the* Benjamin F. Bates *features a painting of Chief Big Foot, legendary leader of the Potawatomi Indians, over the fireplace.*

LEFT: *Owner Peter Bates has the con on the bridge.* — PHOTOS BY R. BRUCE THOMPSON

Western Territories. Benjamin Bates established himself as a farmer in Ohio, and his descendants later migrated farther west to Elmhurst, Illinois. "I thought it would be nice to commemorate the old ship captain's name and at the same time historically commemorate his contribution to the revolution," explains Peter.

"All my life I have had other peoples' boats. I decided for once in my life I did not want to adapt to someone else's idea of what a boat should be. Over the years, I had picked up a lot of ideas about what I wanted. I was keen to build a boat that would have everything I thought a boat should have. This was a purpose-built boat for Lake Geneva. For example, people like to walk around when they are on a boat, so

I planned enough deck space for them to have that freedom. Also, I wished to be able to have a nice meal aboard and to sit down and read the paper. So I included several eating areas with comfortable furniture. But it is designed to go anywhere, down the Mississippi or to Florida. The pilot house can be unbolted and shipped separately for ease of transporting the boat to other bodies of water.

"When I started to design this boat, I didn't have a preconceived notion of what the boat would look like. I knew some of the features I wanted: a pilot house, a saloon with a fireplace, and most importantly, a walk-in engine room where I could have a small machine shop. So I made a scale model of each of these rooms and tried placing them and stacking them in different arrangements to see how they might fit together in an interesting way. I spent about a year building and refining the model. The tugboat style seemed to evolve naturally."

Timothy Graul, the naval architect Peter hired to design the boat, picks up the story: "The *Benjamin F. Bates* is one of the most fascinating design projects I've done. In fact, it was the kind of job I thought every job would be when I decided to be a naval architect. Peter had seen a feature story about Palmer Johnson in the Sunday *Chicago Tribune,* so he called them and they referred him to me. I think Peter drove up to Sturgeon Bay the very next day. Thus began a wonderful relationship. He brought a model with him that he had made that included every detail he wanted in his dream tug, from the puddening fender at the bow to the bridge wings on either side of the boat, from which he could con the boat, to the covered stern lounging area. It was really a pleasure to work with someone so knowledgeable and who had put so much thought into his model. This model was so good-looking that Palmer Johnson put it on display in their lobby.

"While the exterior reflects the tugboat influence, the interior, which began rather modestly, escalated to a real tour-de-force for Palmer Johnson's joinermen. Peter and I spent hours working out various details. True to tugboat tradition, Peter wanted drop windows in the pilot house, so we designed wood-framed windows held up by heavy straps and brass pins, but we used stainless-steel drip pans for them to retract into — century-old technology executed with modern materials.

This cozy below-deck retreat converts into two bunks.
— PHOTO BY R. BRUCE THOMPSON

"The people at Palmer Johnson also sensed that this was a special boat. They put their hearts and souls and all their years of experience into the boat, faithfully executing its rather complex shape. When the boat was launched for sea trials at Sturgeon Bay, it became the lead boat in that year's boat parade.

"I have never before or since worked with a client who enjoyed building a boat as much as Peter did. He became a friend to all of us. He enjoyed coming to Sturgeon Bay, had breakfast and lunch at the local diner, and knowledgeably discussed every detail."

The décor for interior of the yacht was worked out by decorator Jane Plachter-Vogel: "This was a wonderful project, and everyone involved was quite excited about it. We kept Peter's model constantly in the forefront as a guide for all of us. We used dark cherry with brass and green accents in the cabin because the color was so good. Also, we finished it naturally without any stain. That way if it is ever damaged or nicked it can be varnished over and in a short time will attain its original color. Peter wanted to put the painting of Big Foot, legendary chief of the Potowatomi Indians, over the fireplace, so we designed the paneling to accommodate it. We used an antique Dutch ceramic tile around the fireplace. Antique chairs around the dining table and an antique desk in the corner completed the cabin décor. We used marble for the sink countertops. The skylight was a real challenge because Peter wanted it to open. Palmer Johnson custom-made all the mechanism to make it operate."

Peter continues: "Over the years, I collected a variety of whistles and horns that I wanted to use, so I designed an unusually large compressed-air storage capacity. The horns are five-chime Super Typhoons, this particular set coming from the Santa-Fe Railroad's

The engine room, showing the twin Cummins 6-cylinder, 5.9-liter, naturally aspirated 115-horsepower diesel engines with electronic controls. With these engines, the boat easily reaches a hull speed of 14 knots.

— PHOTO BY R. BRUCE THOMPSON

El Capitan passenger train that ran from Chicago to Los Angeles. The deep-throated whistle is from the Ovaltine plant in Villa Park, Illinois, where it signaled the start of the workday at 8 A.M. and the end at 4:30 P.M. Kids from all over town heard that whistle every morning for 50 years and knew they had better get going to school or they would be late. The steering capstan is an antique from Scotland.

"When I began looking at boatbuilders, I settled on Palmer-Johnson as being able to do a first-class job. And did they ever! That yard can make anything. They made flagpoles, cabinets, the table for the saloon. At the end, they suggested teak decks as being the last element to really set the boat apart."

Mechanical features of the boat begin with the twin Cummins model 6BT5.9 6-cylinder, 5.9-liter, naturally aspirated 115-horsepower diesel engines with electronic controls. With these engines, the boat easily reaches the hull speed of 14 knots, with the maneuverability twin engines provide. A 10-kilowatt diesel-electric generator provides ample electrical power. It also has ballast tanks so that 35,000 pounds of water can be taken on for ocean cruising in rough weather. A fire monitor capable of propelling a stream of water over 200 feet was installed for ceremonial use, and also if there were ever a real fire, it would be helpful in putting it out. Radar, depth finder, and a bow-thruster seemed obvious additions to complete the equipment on the boat.

Peter has been a seminal figure in boating on Lake Geneva for over 80 years. Because of his profound interest and study, he has been able to see beyond the ordinary and find or create unusual boats and bring them to the lake for everyone's benefit. He has had the vision to design and the willingness to commit energy and resources to build a memorable yacht. Peter has also been an inspirational figure in the lives of many people. His interest and thoughtful suggestions have guided others. I owe my early interest in Lake Geneva's classic boats to Peter's encouragement and help.

"To end up with exactly the boat you want makes it all worthwhile," Peter adds in conclusion.

Keeping the tradition alive! A rendering of a replica of a traditional 80-foot 1890s clipper-bowed yacht currently under construction. It will be the first of its type to be launched since 1913. — RENDERING BY JOHN WESTMAS

John Porter's Full Throttle *and John Galley's* Silverhawk, *with the latest Kevlar sails set and drawing are closely matched in the first leg of 2001 Sheridan Prize race.* — PHOTO BY R. BRUCE THOMPSON

Chapter 5

PERFORMANCE SAILING

Sailing on Lake Geneva dates from the arrival of the first European settlers in the 1850s. The early sailboats had a distinctly commercial flavor to them, being used for fishing as well as for hauling building materials and staples to the lakeshore residents who were starting to build homes and populate the shoreline.

The first of these commercial sailing craft of any size was the *Fannie Allen*, a two-masted

The gaff-rigged schooner Fannie Allen, *captained by Billy Woods, was one of the earliest sailing vessels on Lake Geneva.*

— PHOTO COURTESY *Beautiful Lake Geneva*

schooner operated by Captain Billy Woods, a bona fide saltwater sea captain and sailing master. He made his living hauling passengers and freight for hire to all parts of the lake. The *Fannie Allen* and her colorful captain became part of the early lore of the lake, and it wasn't long before Billy Woods and other local commercial sailors found themselves pressed into service as experienced hands in competitive sailboat races.

By the early 1870s, following the completion of the Chicago & Northwestern Railroad from Chicago to Lake Geneva, and the 1871 Chicago Fire, Lake Geneva rapidly became a second home for wealthy summer residents, campers, and tourists, and yachting and yacht racing became a genteel if slightly disorganized pastime.

Competitive sailing started as early as 1870 when local residents and vacationers began to see the lake as a means of recreation. The Geneva Lake Regatta Club was formed in 1872. It is safe to say that no two sailboats were alike. The races were sophisticated enough that a handicap system was used, with a time allowance subtracted from each boat's elapsed time, in an effort to give each boat an equal chance of winning. These early races were generally for stakes or cash prizes.

Notable among these early competitive sailors was Julian Rumsey, a commodity trader from Chicago. Rumsey had been mayor of Chicago from 1861–1862 and also president of the Chicago Board of Trade. In 1873, having established a summer home on the eastern shore of Lake Geneva, Rumsey purchased a 21-foot sloop, which he named *Nettie*, from General Ducat, an erstwhile land developer and promoter. This sailboat is memorable because it was fast and also because it had a favorable handicap that enabled it to win virtually every race it entered. The *Nettie* became the model for the famous Sheridan Prize. Years later, in 1892, when the *Nettie* was at the end of her life, Rumsey filled the hull with rock and sank her, lest she be use for any less noble purpose.

The Sheridan Prize

ON AUGUST 27, 1874, Civil War hero General Philip Sheridan, Ulysses Grant's calvary commander, visited Lake Geneva. General Sheridan had made the Union cavalry an effective and respected fighting force. He fought a brilliant campaign in the Shenandoah Valley and, in the last days of the war, Sheridan's force turned Lee's flank and forced the Confederate general to abandon the Richmond area. A few days later, Lee discovered that Sheridan's army lay square across his line of retreat at Appomatox, which led to the end of the war. Of all the principal officers of the war, none had a greater reputation for dashing victory than Philip Sheridan.

His hero status had scarcely diminished in the decade following the war, and the wealthy summer residents vied to entertain their distinguished visitor. The general expressed a desire to see a yacht race, so the hosts decided to name a special race in his honor. The course was to be the length of the lake and return, starting and finishing at the city of Lake Geneva. Two hundred dollars were collected in four days' time, and the renowned silversmiths Giles Brothers, in Chicago, were commissioned to produce a suitable prize. This was a beautifully crafted model of the *Nettie*, at that time the champion sailboat on Lake Geneva.

Nettie won the race on August 31, 1874, and because of the success of the event, the organizers planned to make it an annual regatta to be held on the last day of August each year. Three trustees were put in charge of the prize, and it was widely hoped that General Sheridan would return each year to present the prize.

The Sheridan Prize is still actively sought in serious competition today. Few other sailing prizes in the world have engendered such prestige and enjoyed such a long string of annual contests. Winning the prize is the event of a lifetime and is commemorated by a miniature version of the trophy for the skipper and lapel pins for the crew. The prize has served as guide for organized sailing on Lake Geneva for over 125 years.

The Sheridan Prize, a sterling silver rendition of the gaff-rigged sloop Nettie, *represents one of competitive sailing's oldest competitions.*
— PHOTO BY R. BRUCE THOMPSON

Lake Geneva Yacht Club

ORGANIZED IN 1874, the Lake Geneva Yacht Club can trace its antecedents back to the Geneva Lake Regatta Club. It still embraces the Corinthian principles of that early club and continues a program of organized racing of one-design boats, as it has since the 1900s. The club's racing program has a strong emphasis on the inland scows that have been the main midwestern lakes high-performance sailboat for over hundred years.

Development of the Scow

THE NAME SCOW COMES FROM the Dutch word *schouw*, which describes the broad-beamed, flat-bottom sailboats that traveled the shallow, winding canals of Holland for more than 400 years. They were characterized by their blunt bows and moderate overhang at bow and stern. They often had the double bilge boards still used in scows today.

In this country, scow sailing was promoted in the East during the late 1800s. The biggest impetus to the popularity of scows as racing boats was the 1885 Seawanhaka International Challenge Cup for Small Yachts, held by the Seawanhaka Corinthian Yacht Club, in Oyster Bay, New York. In 1883, the yacht club had implemented a refined measurement formula that took into account both the boat's waterline length and sail area. The intent was that boats built to comply with the rule could be considered essentially equivalent and

With its colorful spinnaker set, Ron Schloemer's *Class A scow* Afterburner *sails downwind.*

— PHOTO BY CINDY O'NEIL

therefore could race without handicaps. This was an early version of one-design class racing. However, the rule favored boats with a larger sail area and a shorter waterline. Because boats with longer waterline have a higher natural speed, the longer boat has an advantage. There was, therefore, a great incentive to design and build boats that exploited the rule by measuring on a short waterline in calm water but sailing on a long waterline when they heeled over. Efforts to exploit this rule led directly to the scow as we know it today. With its flat bottom and blunt bow configuration, the scow has a waterline length when at rest that is about one half its overall length. When sailed heeled over, the rounded bilge becomes immersed for virtually its entire length, effectively doubling the waterline length.

The scow has enjoyed its greatest continuing success on the inland lakes of the Midwest, where the wind and wave conditions have favored its development. The traditional scow classes are Class A (38 feet over all), E (28 feet), C (20 feet), M-20 (20 feet), and M and MC (16 feet). Boats in all of these classes are built to one-design specifications, so the boats are presumed to be equivalent if not identical. The success, then, of any particular boat in winning races should depend on the skill of the skipper and crew. There is no handicap system in these classes. The race starts when the starting gun fires, and the first boat over the finish line wins.

Harry C. "Buddy" Melges, Jr. is currently chairman of Melges Boat Works, Inc., located in Zenda, Wisconsin. He is an internationally known and respected yachtsman who was recently honored by being inducted into the America's Cup Hall of Fame. The official induction ceremony was held in August 2001 on the Isle of Wight, site of the first competition

In national and international competitive sailing, the name Melges is synonymous with winning. Buddy Melges is seen here with his wife, Gloria, his staunchest supporter, surrounded by 50 years of trophies and awards that record a lifetime of achievement. On the wall, over Buddy's right shoulder, are the Olympic bronze and gold medals. On the mantel is the King of Spain trophy. On the table in front are the miniature America's Cup and the Triple Crown World Championship. In the background are miniature versions of the Sheridan Prize.

— PHOTO BY R. BRUCE THOMPSON

Reception for Buddy Melges at the Lake Geneva Yacht Club after the America's Cup victory in 1992. The club was first organized in 1874.
— PHOTO COURTESY MELGES BOAT WORKS

in 1851. Three times in his career, in 1961, 1972, and 1978, Melges was named Yachtsman of the Year. In 1972, he won the Herreshoff Trophy, the United States Sailing Association's most prestigious award, for his outstanding contribution to the sport. He received the W. Van Alan Clark Trophy, the United States Sailing Association's sportsmanship award, in 1986. By that time, he had already won an Olympic bronze medal, Olympic and Pan-American gold medals, world championships in three classes, and three U.S. Men's Sailing Championships.

"This is the lake where I started sailing competitively," Melges remembers. "Billy Grunow and I sailed a C Scow on Lake Geneva in 1949 and won the championship. That launched my sailing career on a

more serious note. That championship and the fact that Melges-built boats were becoming dominant in the scow classes made me realize I could be competitive. With scows, the overall dimensions for length and width of the boat are very specific. What makes a difference is the shape of the bottom, the curve in the bilges and how they fair into the bottom, and the angle of the bottom up to the bow and stern. Melges boats tend to have softer bilges. That's not quite so fast in heavy air, but it moves better in light air.

"The A Scow at 38 feet is about the best type of scow and a wonderful boat to sail. It is as fast as any sailboat and is faster than most. One of the special things about the A Class is the boats are all alike, so it is the sailor who makes a difference. Since 1979, they are all Melges-built boats. No one else builds an A scow today, and we haven't changed the mold since we made it in '79.

"Scow sailing is high-performance sailing, very athletic and physical. There is higher loading of the sheets; it is more of a struggle to manage and to work the boat. You have to be constantly aware of the interaction of the wind and the boat.

"Today I sail for the joy of sailing. It's always nice to win, but I enjoy the race and the competition as much as winning. At 71, I've had a good run in sailing, I can't complain about that.

"I think the most important thing I could tell someone about becoming a good sailor is to present your boat to Mother Nature. Don't wait for Mother Nature to come to you, because it will be too late. You may tip over or worse. Look ahead, read the wind on the water, its speed, its angle, prepare your boat for the wind before you get there. Work with the wind."

Class A Scow

THE CLASS A SCOW is the largest and fastest of the scows. The specifications for this one-design class insist that they be 38 feet long, with an 8-foot-6-inch beam, 1,850 pounds minimum weight, and 550 square feet of working sail area. There are no restrictions on the number or aggregate weight of crew, and most race with six or seven aboard. In *Yachting Magazine's* 1966 One-of-a-Kind Regatta, *Don Quixote*, owned by Don Frankel and Bud Simon, with Bill Bentsen as skipper, was the elapsed-time winner in Division I, beating all of the catamarans.

The Class A scow has been brought to its current state of development through the efforts of many

Buddy and son Harry discuss the latest technology to be incorporated in their boats. Continuous innovation has made Melges boats fast and consistently at the front of the fleet. In the background are the Class A scow molds and the Melges 24 molds.
— PHOTO BY R. BRUCE THOMPSON

people. But since the 1970s, the principal effort has been spearheaded by Melges Boat Works. Gene Trepte recalls the development of the fiberglass A scow: "Prior to 1979, all the Class A boats were made of wood but there was some interest in moving ahead into fiberglass. Bill Perrigo and John Pillsbury worked with Buddy to develop a fiberglass A boat. John Porter

Full Throttle *beating to windward — scow sailing at its best.*

— PHOTO BY R. BRUCE THOMPSON

and I went to the launching when they put the first boat in the water and went for a ride. We thought it performed very well. The rules require 1,850 pounds minimum weight and that glass boat came in around 2,200 pounds, so there was some work to do to get some of the weight out of the boat.

"We worked with Buddy over a period of several years to build two more A boats, and we were able to get the weight down to about 50 pounds under the minimum. We were then able to use lead weights to put weight back into the boat and put it where we wanted it. Each of those boats was fast and won a lot of races. Then John Porter wanted to take the next step, and he had Buddy build him a new A boat using carbon fiber for reinforcement instead of glass fiber.

"I've enjoyed sailing all my life. It is a great sport, with great people. I've enjoyed sailing with my family, with my sons-in-law, and now with my grandchildren. And it's been great to work with Buddy. His son Harry is running the boat works with Andy Burdick, Eric Hood, and Charlie Harrett, and it's a terrific operation."

Owner John Porter comments about *Full Throttle*: "We worked with Buddy Melges and the crew at Melges Boat Works on two earlier glass-fiber-

John Anderson and David Weinberg's Eagle. *It takes many skilled hands to successfully sail a Class A scow.* — PHOTO BY LARRY LARKIN

reinforced polyester-resin A boats and learned a lot about what it takes to build a successful boat. We kept trying to take the weight out of the boat yet keep it as strong as possible to retain its shape and sailing lines in the wave conditions usually encountered in races.

"With *Full Throttle*, I wanted to build the most technologically advanced hull I could using the latest engineered materials and still be within the class rules. To keep the weight down, particularly the weight aloft, we used carbon-fiber reinforcement instead of aluminum in the mast and boom, and also in place of the traditional glass fiber throughout the hull. This gave us a very lightweight hull that was tremendously strong and as stiff as possible, and at the same time gave us the freedom to redistribute the weight required by the class rules while placing it at the optimum locations inside the hull. We were able to change the weight distribution by bringing the weight in from the bow and stern and concentrating it more in the center of the hull. We also spent a great deal of time fairing the hull so the bottom was perfectly smooth and was exactly to the design lines. We did whatever we could to reduce the drag and windage and keep the boat as light as possible."

Class M Scow, Calamity Jane

THE M16 IS A MELGES-DESIGNED scow first built in the early 1950s. Although it is the smallest of the recognized scow classes, it has a substantially following because of its easy handling and responsiveness. The class requires that boats be 16 feet long, with a 5-foot-8-inch beam and a minimum weight of 420 pounds. The boat is sailed with a crew of two.

No sailor is more closely identified with any scow class than Jane Pegel, who has had a long association with the M16s. Since 1960, six boats have carried the name *Calamity Jane*, and most other sailors have read the name from the transom as they followed Jane around the course.

In addition to her achievements at Lake Geneva Yacht Club in Classes C, M, and E, Jane's impressive record in scows includes numerous Inland Lake Yachting

Calamity Jane, an M-16 scow that Jane Pegel made famous by winning virtually every Lake Geneva M-16 trophy at one time or another.
— PHOTO COURTESY JANE PEGEL

Association and Blue Chip titles. At the national level, she won the 1957 and 1964 North American Women's Sailing Championships, the 1974 United States Women's Single-handed Sailing Championship, and was named Yachtswoman of the Year in 1964, 1971 and 1974.

The Geneva Lake Sailing School teaches sailing to aspiring young sailors in Optimist sailing dingys.

— PHOTO COURTESY GENEVA LAKE SAILING SCHOOL

Class E scows, shown on a downwind leg with their colorful spinnakers set, comprise a very competitive class.
— PHOTO BY R. BRUCE THOMPSON

Bob Winter's orange-hulled Blitzkrieg
and John Anderson's Adios, *Sonar Class
keel boats, near the finish line as the
yacht club race committee boat stands by.*
— PHOTO BY R. BRUCE THOMPSON

J-24s, Bohica, *owned by Tony Trajkovich, and*
Spot, *owned by John Mick, participate
in Lake Geneva Yacht Club races.*
— PHOTO BY LARRY LARKIN

Sonar Class

IN RECENT TIMES, the Lake Geneva Yacht Club has provided competitive races for other one-design classes, such as J-24, Laser, X, and Optimist boats. Also among these is the Sonar, which was developed in 1979 by Bruce Kirby. The first boat was brought to Lake Geneva by Jane and Bob Pegel in the spring of 1981. This keelboat is a one-design class with a length of 23 feet and a displacement of 2,100 pounds. The original design was done with the intent of producing a boat that would be fast and able to race but that would also be a good day sailboat for casual sailing. The people behind the concept were all experienced sailors, so there was a clear expectation from the start that the boat would perform well. There are currently more than 15 in the Lake Geneva racing fleet. According to Jane Pegel, "The Sonar is beautifully designed. It sails well to windward — in fact it feels like it wants to go to windward, you don't have to force it. This is a function of the balance of the boat and how the water flows around the fin keel, which in this boat is very efficiently designed. The boat does very well in one-on-one competition with other similar boats, and with breezes over 12 miles per hour, it will win consistently."

Sonar Class sailboats taking their spinnakers in prior to rounding the downwind mark.

— PHOTO BY LARRY LARKIN

Freyja, *owned by Jerry Gutkowski and Peter Arnold, racing in a Great Keel Boat Club event. In the background is John Lincoln's* ZAPT, *a Melges 24 fin-keel boat designed by Reichel & Pugh that incorporates many innovations originally developed for the America's Cup competition.*

— PHOTO BY R. BRUCE THOMPSON

Keelboats

KEELBOATS ON LAKE GENEVA have a wide range of lengths, displacements, and sail areas, hardly any two being alike. The Great Keel Boat Club was founded in 1978 as a means of promoting competition between the different types of keelboats. Because of the variation in design and construction of these boats, some are naturally faster than others. To level the water, so to speak, a handicap system is used so that each boat has an equal chance to win. Initially only one race, known as the Great Keel Boat Race, was held each year, but more races were added to the schedule in succeeding years, and now 25 races are scheduled annually.

Freyja

THE ATTRACTIVE *Freyja*, NAMED for the Nordic goddess of love, is a 33-foot Aphrodite 101, a class of boats built in Denmark. The *Freyja* was originally designed by Elvstrom & Kjaerulff for the King of Denmark, not to any specific rule, but just to sail well. Built around 1978 by the Badvaerft Aps Boat Company and subsequently brought to the United States, it found its way to Lake Geneva in 1980.

According to Jerry Gutkowski, one of the current owners: "We bought this boat because it's a good-looking boat and because it sails well. Although it is quite narrow with a 7 1/2-foot beam, it sails on a long waterline because of the pronounced overhang fore and aft.

"The sail area is finely proportioned with the underwater section of the hull, so the boat is very well balanced. After you set the head sails and main, you can let go of the tiller and the boat will sail itself from one end of the lake to the other. Even in heavy weather, you can trim it up and it goes straight ahead.

Pleasure Sailing and Cruising

IN ADDITION TO ORGANIZED competitive sailing, there is significant pleasure and recreational sailing on Lake Geneva. A wide variety of sailboats can be found. Windsurfers can be seen skimming across the crests of the waves as if carried along by the wind-blown spray from early spring to late fall, when the winds are their gustiest and the sailor the gutsiest. Catamarans, scudding before a freshening breeze, Lasers, Sunfish — they are all here.

Cruising sailboats are seen in all seasons and in all weather conditions. Their white sails and easy motion create a scene reminiscent of the turn of the last century, and it's not hard to imagine the lake populated by such appealing craft. Among the best known is the *Rara Avis*.

It takes experience and savvy to sail close-hauled in a 20-knot wind. Joanne and Paul Lederer are seen here in Rara Avis, their J-34C. — PHOTO BY R. BRUCE THOMPSON

Rara Avis

THE *Rara Avis* HAS BEEN owned by Paul Lederer since it was new in 1990. This model in cruising configuration evolved from Rod Johnstone's J-24 design. It is a fast boat that is well accepted in the racing fraternity yet entirely suitable for cruising. It has a nice balance between a boat designed for performance sailing and a classic cruising design.

When asked about his interest in the J-34C, Paul Lederer responded: "I have always been interested in the beauty of sailing. I spent most of my growing up years on a small inland lake in Michigan. I can remember drawing sailboats, building model sailboats and even rigging a 6-foot dinghy with pontoons and wondering why I could only sail downwind.

"The history of the name *Rara Avis* has its own unique meaning. The dictionary defines *rara avis* as a

Greek mythological bird that can fly on one wing if necessary. The idea that we must all fly on one wing at times has great philosophical meaning to my wife, Joanne, and me. It was *Rara Avis* that set us free from our physical limitations. As our skill in sailing *Rara Avis* in all conditions emerged, we recognized that there were no limits to our experiences, only challenges to our physical inconveniences. *Rara Avis* is more than a boat. It is the fulfillment of dreams, a fantasy actualized."

Henry Bates's Eagle, *a reproduction of an early 1900s Herreshoff design, sailing in front of the Bateses' home on Duck Island.*
— PHOTO BY R. BRUCE THOMPSON

Eagle

OWNED BY HENRY BATES, the traditional 22-foot-long gaff-rigged offshore sloop *Eagle*, with its small cuddy cabin forward, is a replica built in 1970 by Novak Boat Company based on a 1903 Herreshoff design. "There is nothing nicer than a sunset cruise with your family," says Henry. "It gives everyone a chance to enjoy a picnic supper, relax, and experience the easy motion of the boat as the evening breeze gently fills the sail."

Apocalypse, *among the last of the banana spar iceboats, is owned by Bill Sills. It was built by the Johnson Boat Company in White Bear Lake, Minnesota, in 1922, a time when iceboats were converting from gaff-rigged sails to Marconi rigs and the curving spar was believed to be more efficient and, together with the long boom, produce a lower aspect ratio. Bill Sills notes: "Racing this boat is the greatest thrill in sailing. Unlike a Skeeter, which gives a soft, easy ride, an A stern-steerer is always a touch out of control. You guide it along and hope you're OK, but nature has a lot more to say about it than you have. It takes everything you have to sail it in a decent wind and try to win at the same time. It's a greater challenge than any other kind of sailing."*

— PHOTO BY R. BRUCE THOMPSON

Chapter 6

THE ICEBOAT
CENTER OF THE WORLD

There are some who say that the weeks between late December and the middle of March are the best part of the year on Lake Geneva. They refer, of course, to the exhilarating sport of iceboating — a sport all about speed, technology, patience, power, fear, and the edges of control.

The iceboating season on Lake Geneva may be short, but it is long on excitement.

Those who want to experience the fastest ride Mother Nature has to offer must be patient. The ideal day for iceboating requires a convergence of many elements. Few geographical areas provide suitable conditions for sailing on ice. In the United States, parts of the Northeast, the Midwest, and farther west to Montana are located in a band that is cold enough to freeze the lakes and rivers with ice at least four inches thick, with occasional warm spells throughout the winter to periodically melt the accumulated snow and create a glaze on the ice surface. Then the wind must blow at least five miles per hour but not top 25. Snow accumulation of much greater than four inches causes excessive drag on the runners, and if the ice is too smooth or hard, the runners tend to slide. If it is too cold, below 10 degrees Fahrenheit, the wind chill can be devastating.

Lake Geneva's iceboaters monitor a hotline to find out where the ice conditions are good for this most fickle of sports. Intrepid ice sailors sometimes travel hundreds of miles, boat in tow, to find just the right mix of conditions.

The earliest account of iceboating is from Europe and dates from the mid-1600s. The first picture is a woodcut dated 1768 that shows a bluff-bowed, gaff-rigged Dutch sloop with a plank running sideways attached underneath the hull and having a skate runner on each end. Another skate runner is attached to the bottom edge of the rudder hanging over the stern. This creative adaptation of an existing sailboat set the style for stern-steering iceboats for the next 250 years. The Dutch continued to build this type of convertible sailboat for many years, and almost identical examples could be seen in Holland into the 1940s.

Early Days

ICEBOATING WAS BROUGHT TO the United States by the Dutch settlers in the Hudson River Valley as early as 1790. Oliver Booth is generally credited as being the first iceboater in North America, though he pushed what was little more than a box with skates in each corner onto the frozen Hudson River at Poughkeepsie, New York. By the mid-1800s, New York and particularly the Hudson River had become the center of iceboating in North America. Development was rife as designers and builders found new ways to build stronger and lighter craft, using flexible planks, hollow backbones, and wire stays to secure the components in place.

Believing that bigger was faster, ever larger and more hugely canvassed stern-steering ice yachts were launched, culminating in the largest of them all, the 69-foot *Icicle* carrying 1,070 square feet of sail. It was built in 1869 by Jacob Buckhout, the outstanding iceboat designer and builder of the era, for Commodore John E. Roosevelt, founder of the Hudson River Ice Yacht Club. The *Icicle* was constructed of planks sawn from trees cut on the Roosevelt estate. She was transported

In the seventeenth century, the Dutch figured out how to make a sailboat into an ice boat by fastening a plank sideways under the hull with a skate runner on each end.

— DRAWING BY JOHN WESTMAS

to the Hudson River on a railroad flatcar, and for a while, she was the most formidable boat on the river. She is owned today by the Franklin Delano Roosevelt Library in Hyde Park and is currently an exhibit at New York's Hudson River Maritime Museum in Kingston, though there was talk a few years ago about getting her back on the ice.

Iceboating, like sailing, became a sport for the wealthy. No expense was spared to build a bigger boat to outsail a rival. Professional crews manned the boats, and speeds approached 100 miles per hour. Not content to race each other, the Hudson River ice sailors challenged the Chicago Express, which ran on tracks along the Hudson between Poughkeepsie and Ossining, New York — usually winning.

Beginning in 1902, icebreakers started keeping the Hudson River open all winter for commercial navigation, so the areas of greatest iceboating activity shifted to other localities in the Northeast and to the inland lakes of Wisconsin, Minnesota, and Michigan. Information about developments on the Hudson River had already spread to Wisconsin well before the turn of the century, where they found fertile breeding grounds.

Sailors and supporting crew who love iceboating gather for the competition and camaraderie that run deep in the sport.

— PHOTO BY R. BRUCE THOMPSON

Because stern-steerers have a tendency to spin out of control if the steering runner lifts off the ice or the skipper rounds a mark too sharply, sailors in a number of areas began experimenting with the concept of a front-steering boat in the interest of better control. In 1932, Walter Beauvais, in collaboration with Harry Melges, in Williams Bay, Wisconsin, took an important step. He designed and built what he called the Beau-Skeeter, a 13-foot front-steering iceboat with 75 square feet of sail. He put it on Lake Geneva and changed the sport.

Although front-steering iceboats had been built earlier, notably by Starke Meyer of Pewaukee,

Wisconsin, this boat was a major breakthrough. Instead of the traditional main sail and jib, it featured a single sail secured to a mast that was raked aft at an angle of 15 degrees. The boat was designed so that the pressure of the wind on the sail forced the bow-steering runner more firmly onto the ice instead of lifting the steering runner off the ice, as is the case with stern-steerers. The name Skeeter is generally believed to be from the slang term for mosquito, and many Skeeters still have the mosquito insignia in their sail.

The following year, Williams Bay sailors started the Beau-Skeeter Ice Boat Club, which was renamed the Skeeter Ice Boat Club (SIBC) in 1938. From that point on, racing on Lake Geneva was held under the aegis of the SIBC and the Northwestern Ice Yachting Association, established in 1912. The racing rules for the sport are governed by the National Ice boat Authority.

To satisfy sailors who wanted a good race without the demands of expensive development, Skeeters started competing in early 1940s in three divisions: Class A, which remained open to experimentation, with only the 75-square-foot sail area limitation; Class B, which was composed mostly of the 25-foot-long side-by-side two-seater model designed in the 1930s by Ted Mead, and further developed in the 1950s by

Walworth cabinetmaker Bill Boehmke into what he called a Boe-craft; and Class C, which had a mast height restriction of 20 feet.

Today, Lake Geneva is home to a variety of iceboat classes and types that whoosh, rattle and roar up and down the lake. From a distance, there seems to be a certain sameness to most iceboats, but nothing could be further from the truth. Most modern iceboats are derivatives of the Skeeter type, such as the sporty and internationally popular 12-foot DN, the spirited Renegade, the Nite, and the newly developed M-80, but the undisputed kings of the fleet are the majestic Class A iceboats, the Hudson River-type stern-steerers.

Renegade Class iceboats line up for the start of another race. — PHOTO BY R. BRUCE THOMPSON

Skeeters

THE LIGHTNING-FAST A SKEETER is an open design class with only a few rules that relate to the sail area, defined from the beginning as 75-square-foot maximum, and how it is measured, but no limits on the size of the boat. The Skeeter has undergone a remarkable evolution in the endless search for speed, with hulls getting longer, improved suspension of the runners, cockpits moving first aft of the runner plank then forward of the mast, and the increasing use of high-tech construction materials. These are the thoroughbreds of the sport, being the fastest non-motorized vehicles known to man. Skeeters have logged some impressive records. A Skeeter was clocked at 143 miles per hour on Lake Geneva, and speeds upwards of that have been claimed. Wind-chill factors take on special meanings at high speeds and every square inch of skin must be protected. For safety reasons, the SIBC requires competitors to wear safety helmets, and racing is not permitted when the temperature is below 10 degrees Fahrenheit.

Buddy Melges is a lifelong Skeeter sailor, having started in 1936, when he was six years old. By that time, he had already sailed in the summer, so he knew about the wind, and he'd been taken for rides on the ice in his father's side-by-side. During that winter, Buddy sailed off by himself for the first time in the 16-foot Beau-Skeeter *Mickey Finn* and started an iceboating career that has never slowed down. Today, Melges races both his 40-foot stern-steerer *Ferdinand*

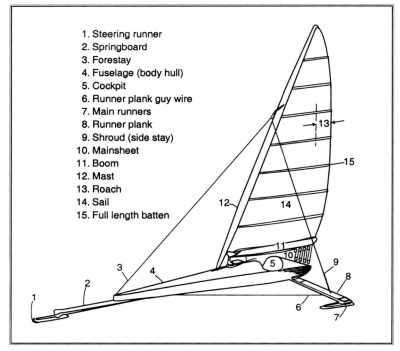

1. Steering runner
2. Springboard
3. Forestay
4. Fuselage (body hull)
5. Cockpit
6. Runner plank guy wire
7. Main runners
8. Runner plank
9. Shroud (side stay)
10. Mainsheet
11. Boom
12. Mast
13. Roach
14. Sail
15. Full length batten

Principal parts of a Skeeter.
— DRAWING BY JOHN WESTMAS

and a very fast 30-foot A Skeeter called *Honeybucket XI*, built in 1995 by Bill Mattison in Madison. He wins big in both.

Honeybucket XI is a further development of the Dan Clapp-designed front-cockpit Skeeters that started to stun the class in the early 1990s. About 30 feet overall, her hull is sitka spruce with a carbon-fiber skin; the runner plank and springboard are sitka spruce; the mast is carbon fiber.

"My father collaborated with Walter Beauvois in developing the Skeeter in the 1930s. The rules for the Skeeter are pretty simple: 75 square feet of sail, 12-inch roach. But more engineering and mechanics are involved. The runner blades, the leading edge, the

Buddy Melges and his Bill Mattison-built Skeeter Honeybucket XI *in a hike as it rounds a mark and begins to accelerate.* — PHOTO BY R. BRUCE THOMPSON

suspension, are all constantly being refined and improved, as well as the flexibility and stiffness of the runner plank and backbone. You have to work on these constantly to improve your speed. There are iceboaters who don't sail during the summer. They spend their time adjusting and refining their iceboat to make it go faster, to be more competitive. They work on their runners to have them in perfect shape, they work on the runner plank to make its stiffness just right, and they work on their sails to reshape them.

"The skills are different for iceboating. In summer sailing, you pay more attention to the wind. If the wind shifts three or five or seven degrees, you tack in response. In iceboating, you're going so fast you may not pick up the wind shift and you may sail through the shift before you can respond. You sail a diamond pattern between the leeward mark and the windward mark, sailing 35 to 40 degrees to the true wind angle, depending on ice conditions and with a good wind. If the wind falls off, you have to open up that angle. If you get a lift, you take advantage of it by altering your course. If you get a header, you can tack for advantage.

"These boats go over a 100 miles per hour on hard ice. Even with a wind of 10 miles per hour, you can go 75 miles per hour, over seven times the speed of the wind. In iceboating, you're going so fast against your competition you can fly right by."

Watching Buddy sail in the *Honeybucket XI* is like watching a concert master. He leans forward, fully involved with the boat. Other sailors lean back against the backrest in their seats, but Buddy is working the boat, feeling the boat's movements in response to the wind and ice, playing off the surges to build speed, and constantly urging the boat forward. Melges won the Class E (Skeeter) title at the 2001 Northwestern Ice Yachting Association Regatta and Division A at the International Skeeter Association Regatta in March. These earned him the Triple Crown Trophy top performance in the two events combined and the Senior Trophy for sailors over 50.

On the Rocks VI

WITH ITS BRIGHT RED HULL and blond spars, Birdell "Burly" Brellenthin's *On the Rocks VI* is a well-known sight on Lake Geneva's ice. The boat is considered to be over 50 years old, but its exact age depends on what part you're looking at. As is common in iceboating, *On the Rocks VI* is a composite of pieces of many boats. Her precise provenance is challenging.

All of Burly's *On the Rocks* have been B Skeeters. There are very specific requirements for this one-design class. Boats must have 75 square feet of sail area, and the hull, mast step location, runner plank, spar and boom all have specific dimensions, all precisely determined, but with some tolerance.

Burly started iceboating in the 1930s and has been racing since 1947, when he and Gene Liechty had a Johnson stern-steerer named *Dorla*: "I've been iceboating since I was ten years old. I was fascinated by these boats as a kid. I started going down to the ice when the lake first froze and helped assemble the iceboats, hoping that someone would offer me a ride. I sailed every weekend I could and even went down late in the day after school to try to get some sailing in with Gene Liechty and Hink Morgan in the *Blue Bird*, a small stern-steerer.

"Shortly after World War II was over, I had saved up enough money and bought my first iceboat, a little single-seat Skeeter I named *Winter Squaw*. It was a home-built boat that had a number of previous owners. In fact, it is still around today.

Burly Brellenthin in his On the Rocks VI, *a Boehmke-built side by side.* — PHOTO BY R. BRUCE THOMPSON

"After a few years, I was able to get a bigger and better boat and eventually worked my way up to a side-by-side built by Bill Boehmke. This is a great boat because it is fast enough to be very competitive, but you can also take someone with you for more casual sailing. I have taken many people out for rides over the years who enjoyed the sport so much they eventually bought their own boat.

"Boehmke was a real craftsman, the premier builder of the side-by-side. He was very meticulous in building his boats, and because of the care he took,

most of the 75 boats he built are still in existence today. He wouldn't build a boat unless he had an order, so there weren't that many built.

"I enjoy iceboating because of the speed and the competition. It is great to feel the boat accelerate and reach those tremendous speeds. And you really have to work at it to be competitive. It can be below zero and you still work up a sweat."

Helping sailors to enjoy themselves and ensuring that their races are structured and well run is of big interest to Burly, and he has devoted his energies to the organizational aspects of the sport for more than 50 years. He remembers a freezing regatta off Fontana — "brutal," he called it — and right after that came a rule banning racing in temperatures below 10 degrees.

Burly's enthusiasm for iceboating is boundless and contagious, and as he says, "It helps pass the winter so fast." He is a regular on the ice with SIBC's ATV, setting courses, starting races, ensuring that

sailors have the help they need, both to get out to the race course and, at the end of a season, to get off the ice in a safe and timely fashion. He recently retired as chairman of the Skeeter Ice Boat Club Sailing Committee, though he is sure to be there when needed, and he remains as a member of the Ice Checkers, the group that gathers key information about the lake for the Ice Boater's Hot Line.

Intensely competitive, B Skeeters Bottoms Up, *owned by Dan Janikowski, and* Blitz'n, *sailed by George Beukema, race blade to blade with sails trimmed home and windward runners off the ice in a hike.* — PHOTO BY R. BRUCE THOMPSON

At home on hard or soft water, Jane Pegel has excelled in both winter and summer sailing. — PHOTO COURTESY JANE PEGEL

DN

THIS CLASS OF ICE BOATS WAS STARTED in the mid-1930s, a product of a Detroit News (DN) design competition. The contest was won by Archie Arroll, Joe Lodge, and Norman Jarrett. Their design is a direct descendant of the Skeeter type, a front-steering boat with a single sail and raked mast. It is not strictly a one-design class, but there are limitations on the size: the 12-foot length, the 8-foot plank, the 16-foot maximum mast height, and the 60-square-foot sail area. It has become the biggest class worldwide, with over 10,000 boats officially registered, 5,000 in North America alone, and many more built for casual non-competitive sailing. One if its major appeals is that it is an inexpensive boat to build and simple enough that you can build it yourself. Kits are available with everything you need to build your own. The DN is a fast boat that has become increasingly faster over the years.

The DN class is proud of its Lake Geneva sailors. Mike O'Brien has won three world championships, and Jane Pegel continues to be a contender. If Jane had to chose between sailing in the winter or the summer, winter would win hands down, no hesitation. This might seem surprising coming from a "summer sailor" who has among her titles U.S. Yachtswoman of the Year and probably has more trophies than most small yacht clubs, but Jane is a true iceboating aficionado.

Jane started iceboating on Lake Geneva as a teenager in 1947, in a 20-foot Mead-designed Skeeter. Only two things have kept her off the ice since then: weather and motherhood. She stayed with the Skeeter Class until the boat became too hard to handle — "They went downwind faster than I care to go" — and in 1956 she took up the DN, which was new to the Skeeter Ice Boat Club that year. She celebrated the occasion by becoming SIBC's first DN champion, and in 1960 was the first woman to win the DN Class

Annual Regatta, later called the National Championship. She won the national title again in 1963 and has numerous Northwestern Ice Yachting Association titles to her credit, and Jane finds the boat both a challenge and pleasure to sail. The best weather? Jane likes a 10-to-12-mile-per-hour breeze and ice with a little texture for better control. "Glass ice," she says, "is hard to hang onto. You can feel the ice right through the runners and the hull. And the boat is very responsive. You can feel it accelerate as you trim the sail. It takes more skill and the right touch to sail it well, but once you have the fundamentals down, it just zips along. It has phenomenal performance. You can make it dance on the ice. The boat feels like it is part of you."

Besides campaigning her DN, her sixth to date, Jane is the voice of the Skeeter Ice Boat Club, serving both as editor of its newsletter and producer of its hotline, a taped telephone message that runs from December to March, informing sailors about conditions on the lake and the location of regattas. She also chairs the SIBC's ice-checking committee, whose members collectively spend about 40 hours a week studying the lake from a car or a boat or on foot, measuring the thickness of the ice and locating holes, seams, and potential trouble spots. It is a service critical to every sailor's safety and enjoyment.

With the sail trimmed and clear ice ahead, Taku *gets underway.*
— PHOTO BY R. BRUCE THOMPSON

The largest operating iceboat in the world, the magnificent Deuce *,*
traveling a mile a minute with owner Rick Hennig and Todd Knop aboard . — PHOTO BY R. BRUCE THOMPSON

Deuce

THE *Deuce* IS CURRENTLY THE largest operating iceboat in the world. At 54 feet 6 inches in length, and with a 36-foot-wide runner plank, 51-foot-high mast rising to 54 feet off the ice, and carrying 750 square feet of sail, it is hard to find enough superlatives to describe the boat.

It is owned today by Rick Hennig, a lifelong iceboat sailor and many-time champion. It was during a sail on *Ferdinand* in the 1980s, with Harry Melges at the helm, that Rick Hennig first contracted stern-steerer fever: "As far as sailing a big stern-steerer goes, I remember when I got excited about them. I went out sailing on *Ferdinand*, Buddy Melges's Class A stern-steerer, with Buddy's son Harry, about 25 years ago. That was the ride of a lifetime. The feeling of power — not sure who or what was in control, if we were steering or if the wind was taking us almost unpredictably to the edge, like a runaway locomotive roaring out of control, with deafening sound and fury down the ice, with no track. I knew I was going to have one of these magnificent boats."

The Deuce *bow cap was fabricated from stainless steel and then polished to a mirror-like finish.*
— PHOTO BY R. BRUCE THOMPSON

The mast step and mast base were machined from a solid billet of aluminum by a computer-controlled milling machine, with the nam laser cut.

The massive size of the runners and the strength of the supporting hardware are testaments to the tremendous forces involved in iceboat racing.
— PHOTOS BY R. BRUCE THOMPSON

The *Deuce* was designed and built in the early 1930s by Joe Lodge, who was one of the three designers of the little DN in Detroit. It was commissioned by Clare Jacobs, inventor of the Jacobs chuck, which has been used almost universally for hand drills and drill presses since that time.

The *Deuce* was purchased by Rick Hennig in 1995. As Rick remembers, "It was a real basketcase. As I look back at it, I don't know if I would have purchased it if I had known what was going to be involved. We ended up opening up the spruce backbone, putting in new bulkheads, regluing, refastening, and reinforcing everything.

"The state of the hardware was the biggest problem. There wasn't enough left of it from rust and corrosion so you could safely sail the boat. We fabricated most of it from scratch, cutting stainless-steel plates, then welding them together and polishing them. That's how we fabricated the bow and stern ends to the backbone. The mast step was CNC milled out of a solid block of aluminum. We used a laser to cut the script on the mast step."

Rick Hennig campaigns his boat with Todd Knop. After competing in the 2001 Hearst and Stuart events, they went on to win the overall championship in the Class A division in both Northwestern Ice Yachting Regatta and the Wisconsin stern-steerer event.

This restored prize-winning 1956 De Havilland Beaver model DH3, powered by a 450-horsepower Pratt & Whitney radial engine, belongs to John Melk. A versatile amphibian aircraft, the Beaver cruises at 120 knots and can land on land, water, or, with skis attached to the wheels, on ice and snow.

— PHOTO BY JAMES HANNY

EVERY ICEBOATER SAVORS SPECIAL MOMENTS. Stern-steerer skipper Bill Bentsen talks of the windward mark rounding and the excitement of the acceleration downwind as the boat's speed roughly doubles. B-Skeeter veteran Burly Brellenthin talks of the thrill of the ride and his boat's amazing maneuverability. Jane Pegel talks of the satisfaction she gets from sailing her DN, especially when conditions are perfect. As she puts it, "You just lie back and go."

"I'd give up a whole season of summer racing on Lake Geneva for a week of good iceboating," says Buddy Melges. It's just that kind of sport.

Kishwauketoe, the Lake of Sparkling Water, still sparkles today and includes
a kaleidoscope of activities on, above, and under its shimmering surface. — PHOTO BY CULLY PILLMAN

Chapter 7

KISHWAUKETOE IN THE 21st CENTURY

The unique depth and clearness of Geneva Lake, the result of glacial moraines created tens of thousands of years ago, together with the natural beauty of the surrounding shoreline, create an idyllic setting for recreation and relaxation. It is not surprising that Lake Geneva has been a destination for visitors for over a 150 years.

While the earliest Native people made use of canoes for hunting and fishing and moving around the lake, there was an obvious need for improved waterborne transportation with no developed roads around the lake so waterborne transportation was a necessity. As early as 1849, the first commercial enterprise was established under the impressive name of the Geneva Lake Commerce and Navigation Company to assist residents and visitors in navigating the lake and promoting trade.

Today, the Geneva Lake Cruise Line continues the longstanding tradition of daily narrated lakeshore tours from early April through October. Special cruises are also offered with historical commentaries on the history of the lake, including biographical sketches of the industrial pioneers who built palatial estates around the shoreline engendering the name "Newport of the West."

Lady of the Lake

THE *Lady of the Lake*, CHRISTENED in the summer of 1963, was the first significant vessel to be built since the 1920s and the first truly large double-deck boat to be launched since 1892. The design captures the essence of the original 1873 *Lady of the Lake* while using the latest materials and technology in the construction.

The hull measures 60 feet long and 18 feet wide, and was fabricated by Dubuque Boat & Boiler Co. at Dubuque, Iowa. With the addition of the sternwheel and walkways, the overall size increased to 90 feet long and 24 feet wide. The superstructure, woodwork and machinery were installed by Gage Marine at their boatyard in Williams Bay. The décor and trim were styled by Brooks Stevens, a leading industrial designer of the era, from Milwaukee, Wisconsin. The vessel was furnished with the appropriate period accessories that created the feel of a late nineteenth century steamboat.

The Lady of the Lake remains one of the best-recognized symbols of the Lake Geneva area and is used throughout the season for excursions, weddings, business outings, and private parties.

Tom Gilding creatively portrays Mark Twain on historic Lake Geneva tours aboard the Lady of the Lake, *announcing points of interest and providing commentary in Twain's vernacular.* — PHOTO BY MARY GILDING

AT RIGHT: *The* Lady's *upper deck is a picturesque and popular location for wedding toasts. Newlywed couple Amy and Dave Tanking celebrate their marriage with friends Kristin and John Larkin.*
— PHOTO BY R. BRUCE THOMPSON

Walworth II

DATING BACK TO THE 1870S, many years before there was a reliable road system around Lake Geneva, mail, newspapers, and sundries were delivered by boat to lakeshore residents. In the earliest days, small steam launches were used, but in 1916 the first *Walworth* was built. It was named for the county in which Lake Geneva resides. This 75-foot wood-planked vessel faithfully carried the mail for over 50 years and became known simply and affectionately as "the mail boat."

By the mid 1960s, the first *Walworth* had exceeded its economic life, and the decision was made to build a replacement. In 1965, the *Walworth II* was launched. This steel-hulled vessel was built by Schwartz Marine in Two Rivers, Wisconsin. With an original length of 60 feet and a 14 foot beam, the boat displaced 17 tons and had a carrying capacity of 150 passengers.

When we built the *Walworth II*, it was out of necessity, and we didn't have the time or resources to make her as aesthetically attractive as we wanted. We believed that we could make some changes to improve the lines and create a more attractive vessel. We looked at examples of European lake and river excursion boats and tried to give the *Walworth II* the most sleek and graceful styling possible. I am very proud of the work everyone did on that project.

The *Walworth II*, still known throughout the area as "the mail boat," continues the tradition of marine mail delivery on the only remaining marine delivery route of its type in the country. Loaded with passengers,

Mail girl Sue Couffer on delivery. Early summer tryouts are held for candidates, who must to show their athletic prowess for this special delivery job. — PHOTO BY JEAN COUFFER

The Jim Riley family dog, Maize, dutifully fetches the morning paper as mail girl Jen Griffing stretches on a swing-by delivery. — PHOTO COURTESY GENEVA CRUISE LINES

mail, and a very agile mail carrier, the *Walworth II* departs every morning between June 15 and September 15 to deliver the mail to the piers of more than 50 lakeshore homes. This daily cruise is popular because the boat travels near the shore, allowing passengers a close-up view of lakeshore estates, and also because of the unique way the mail is delivered. Its arrival is eagerly anticipated by lakeshore residents and children run to the dock to greet the mail boat.

To deliver the mail, the mail carrier must jump from the front of the *Walworth II* to the pier, deposit the mail in the pier mailbox, pick up outgoing mail, and then leap back on the stern before the boat has departed. Speed and agility are necessary for this job, because the mail boat doesn't stop. There are occasional wet deliveries, but Neill Frame, captain of the *Walworth II* for more than 30 years, has never lost a letter.

The Belle of the Lake *was built in 1972 as a recreation of a classic lake steamer from the late nineteenth century.*
The Belle, *as she is fondly called, offers dinner cruises, Dixieland band tours, and ice-cream socials.* — PHOTO BY BILL GAGE JR.

Belle of the Lake

WITH THE SUCCESSFUL RETURN of the *Lady of the Lake*, in 1963 Gage Marine decided to build another new excursion boat, the *Belle of the Lake*. Bill Gage was adamant that the new boat incorporate many of the traditional elements of turn-of-the-century double-deck steamers and look like a classic lake steamboat of the late nineteenth century. According to Bill: "We wanted the boat to be traditional in design and historically authentic to something that would have been on the lake during the steamboat era. We wanted a double-decker, but since we already had built one paddlewheeler, we wanted to create something more along the lines of the *Lucius Newbury*, but without the sidewheel, or like the *Harvard*, but with a front pilot house, and with clean lines and a graceful stern.

Many details from earlier boats were incorporated in the *Belle*, including the smooth, rounded fantail stern. The gradual flare of the sheer running forward to meet the vertical or "plumb" bow was a subtle, but important detail. The large curved panels that swoop down from the bow toward the deck were a feature seen on a steamboat on the Bodensee in Germany. An antique brass anchor windlass salvaged from the Porter yacht *Whileaway* adds another accent to the bow.

The attractive double-decker was 65 feet long and 18 feet abeam when launched in 1972. The basic hull was fabricated by Dubuque Boat & Boiler Co., while Gage Marine built the entire superstructure in Williams Bay. A number of modifications have been made since completion. In 1985, the hull was lengthened and the funnel enlarged, thereby improving the proportions and enhancing the traditional lines.

The *Belle*, as the vessel is popularly known, has been fitted out for complete food service and offers luncheon and dinner service for 130 people as well as cruises for up to 225 people. A live Dixieland band can be provided and daily afternoon ice-cream socials are popular with all ages.

On the upper deck of the Belle, *Julie Griffing serves young friends Connor, Cricket, Sean, and Kelly as they share one of life's sweetest pleasures, ice cream on the lake*

— PHOTO BY R. BRUCE THOMPSON

Officially designated as a Model DUKW-353, 2.5-ton 6 x 6 amphibian truck by the U.S. Army during World War II, these amphibious vehicles, popularly known as DUCKS, participated in many military operations. Of the 20,000 originally built, the surviving few have become collector's items. This one, in authentic original condition, has been in the Larkin family for four decades as a parade float, for trekking with friends, and for transporting wedding parties.

— PHOTO BY VIRGIL WUTTKE

Two of Lake Geneva's intrepid adventurers, Cully Pillman and W. J. Goes, prepare to descend to the 140-foot depths of Lake Geneva in their two-man sport submarine, in search of antiquities and marine life. The rated depth of the submarine is 150 feet, and traveling at 5 knots, it has the ability to stay underwater for two and a half hours. It was previously used in filming the movie The Hunt for Red October. *Says Cully, "It is a totally different experience. We are conquering a whole new world, like an adventure no one has done before, going 140 feet below the surface with time to see things illuminated clearly with electric lights, time to look at carefully at them, and time to talk about them because our heads are out of the water. And there is only one of these, so there is no traffic to contend with."* — PHOTO BY LARRY LARKIN

Mickey Finnegan prefers getting his daily exercise on his Hydro-Bike. This modern recreation of earlier pedal boats is the Explorer I model, measuring 10 feet long and weighing 125 pounds. Top speed is 10 miles per hour, but normal cruising speed, requiring about 1/10 horsepower from the rider, is in the 6 to 7 mile per hour range. — PHOTO BY LARRY LARKIN

Boat Day and Beyond

WHILE TRADITIONAL BOATING ABOUNDS, the lake is also host to a variety of other ways to enjoy its deep blue water. Many recreational activities and watercraft have evolved, catalyzed by the quality of the water. Indeed, thrilling water sports thrive underwater while an assortment of watercraft race over the surface.

In July, "Boat Day" begins at the Abbey Marina for nearly 300 pediatric cancer patients who are participants in One-Step-at-a-Time Summer Camp at the Lake Geneva Campus of Aurora University. The boats cruise to Big Foot Beach and, upon arrival, form a semi-circle breakwater to create a protective basin for the young people to enjoy water games. At the end of the day, everyone returns to the harbor for a barbecue dinner and a take-home bag of memories. The volunteers all agree that they get back much more than they give.

— PHOTO BY HARRY NELSON